The Grandmother Legacies

Compiled By:

Rebecca Hall Gruyter
International Best Selling Author

COPYRIGHT 2017 ALL RIGHTS RESERVED

NO PART OF THIS PUBLICATION MAY BE REPRODUCED, STORED IN A RETRIEVAL SYSTEM, OR TRANSMITTED IN ANY FORM OR BY ANY MEANS, ELECTRONIC, MECHANICAL, PHOTOCOPY, RECORDING, OR ANY OTHER WITHOUT THE PRIOR PERMISSION OF THE AUTHOR

Table of Contents

Foreword 5
ABOUT THE COMPILER 11
ACKNOWLEDGEMENTS 13
Legacies of Great Courage & Strength 14
SHIFTING SANDS 15
By: Renée Sands
LEGACY OF COURAGE SOARING WITH DRAGONS 24
By: Victoria C. Leo
LIVE WITHOUT RESERVATIONS 34
By: Colleen Sandra Quinn
CONNECTION AND CELEBRATION 43
By: Catherine M. Laub
HONORING MY FEMININE ROOTS 51
By: Danielle Nistor
Legacies of Connection, Intention and Purpose .. 58
PROFOUND IMPRINTS 59
By: Susan State
MOTHERED FROM A DISTANCE 67
By: Trisha Garrett
MY FAVORITE HEALER GRANDMA TINA 77
By: Lorraine Giordano

THE INFAMOUS ONE: ON BEYOND THE MAGIC
GRANDMA 82

By: Nina Price
ACTIONS SPEAK LOUDER THAN WORDS 89
By: Pamala Hunter Smith
STRONG AND INDEPENDENT WOMEN, A LEGACY 96
By: Kerry Hargraves
Legacies of Great Joy and Love 106
STIRRING UP LOVE 107
By: Mary E. Knippel
CHILDHOOD SAFE HAVENS: GRANDMA ROSE &
EXPRESSIVE ART 116
By: Trina Swerdlow
WISDOM OF LIFE WITH GRANDMA NETTIE 130
By: Angela Blaha
VORACIOUSLY CURIOUS THE ART OF DEEPENING
CONNECTIONS 138
By: Kiml Avary
MY LOVING LIGHT FILLED GRANDMOTHER 146
By: Barbara Gross
HOMESTEADING IN NORTH DAKOTA 153
By: Sandra Edwards
THANK YOU NOTE FROM THE COMPILER 160
CLOSING THOUGHTS 162
REVIEWS..183

Foreword
"The Grandmother Legacies"
By: Rebecca Hall Gruyter, Book Compiler

Thank you for leaning into "The Grandmother Legacies." I'm honored and excited to bring this powerful book to you, featuring over 15 legacy stories that will touch your heart, lift your spirits, and we hope inspire you to create and share your legacy stories and perhaps even start a legacy of your own.

Thank you, Teresa Hawley-Howard from Woman on a Mission (WOM) Publishing wanted to publish a book for us. WOM leaned in to the heart and vision of bringing multiple heart-centered authors and experts together to share their respective legacy stories.

As the Compiler, I am so honored and proud to bring this amazing group of authors that represents three generations of women sharing their legacy stories and messages; this rich multi-generation collection of experts share powerfully from a multi-generation perspective.

Granddaughters sharing about their grandmothers, mothers sharing about their mothers and the legacy they hope to pass on, and even Grandmothers richly sharing their own legacies and all that they hope to pass on to their family and future generations.

Celebrating and sharing our Grandmother Legacies is close to my heart my Grandmothers (all four of them) richly blessed and impacted me. They had such a great impact on my life that it inspired the desire to create this book.

I believe it is important that we lift up and honor our Grandmothers. They have had and are having a powerful multi-generational impact that I believe needs to be seen, heard, shared, and celebrated.

I was blessed to have four Grandmothers in my life…all unique, powerful and wonderfully made women who greatly impacted my life and have inspired the shape and form of the empowerment work that I now get to do in the world. I now get to lift others up, giving them platforms to reach more people sharing the gifts, talents, and messages they are called to bring forth and share with the world.

The greatest gift my grandmothers gave me, was the gift of walking beside me sharing their heart, life, and experience and wisdom with me. They shared with me from the perspective of both as my Grandmother and as a woman. **I'm so thankful that they were willing to share their heart, life and journey with me.** I will always be thankful for and am truly blessed to have and have had each of them in my life.

My Grandmothers taught me so much and in fact when I started my empowerment work, their stories and the wisdom and lessons they taught me were a popular subject for radio interviews, TV shows, live stages and podcasts. Our Grandmother stories are truly a powerful gift in our life. I will be sharing my own Grandmother Stories in a book to be released soon (coming in 2018…so stay tuned). But as I was creating it, others came forward with a calling on their heart to share their Grandmother Legacy stories too…so I honor and celebrate these powerful legacy messages and stories that have been called forth and am deeply honored and humbled to be entrusted with them and to now get to share them with you.

Before we lean into enjoy these powerful chapters, I wanted to take just a moment to share and acknowledge my wonderful Grandmothers and to thank them for being willing to share the gift of who they were both as Grandmothers and as women. I wanted to acknowledge and thank my Grandmothers for being part of my life and inspiring both my own Grandmother Stories book to be published in 2018 and this powerful Grandmother Legacies Anthology. All of my Grandmothers walked in great love, believed in the sacredness of life, and the deep respect of others and of God. I'm thankful for their legacy and the gift of having them in my life.

My Grandmother Guarascio taught me to discover where I start and stop; to not wait for permission. But instead, be willing to discover where you start and stop and share the gift of who you are authentically and powerfully.

My Grandmother Quinn taught me to pause and take a breath…. allow myself to fully process both the highs in life and the lows in life on a cellular level and to remember to always take care of myself…in fact to give myself grace, love and understanding just like we would for our very best friend. To live deeply, love fully and allow yourself to be fully loved. She also taught me that the parts of others she found most beautiful and wonderful were their quirks, their differences and even imperfections made them even more beautiful and loveable.

My Grandmother Ives taught me the importance of lifting others up and that we can all make a positive difference heart by heart and life by life. She also taught me how to make the flower pens that I frequently share at my live event. Each pen representing the beautiful and unique flower we each are in the garden of life. She also taught me to enjoy learning, growing and that it's about celebrating the process all along the way.

My Grandmother Hall shared her legacy of walking with honor and integrity. She taught me to be willing to work hard for what truly matters to you. I also share her love of books and reading. She also shared with me the gift of her laughter…I hear her echoed out in the way that I laugh and am thankful to carry her with me in every laugh.

They taught me so much about life, love, how to be present and walk powerfully in the world.

I'm thankful to them and want to encourage you to embrace the truths and wisdom they taught me: Be willing to discover where you truly start and stop. Be

willing to share the gift of who you are with the world. Remember to take care of yourself; treating yourself with great love, grace, and understanding. Be willing to bloom fully and lift others up. Remember to share your joy with others and be willing to work hard when needed and walk in the way of truth and full alignment of who you are and are called to be.

In creating this book, I asked each heart-centered and powerful co-author to share some of their Grandmother Legacy Stories. I'm so proud of what each co-author has shared in their chapters, and am honored to have each of them leaning in to share their powerful and rich legacy stories and messages. I am equally honored that you have said "yes" to our book and know you will get great value out of the journey through its pages. Your heart will be touched, spirit inspired, and I believe your walk will be enriched by what you will experience in each chapter.

Now it's your turn. Are you going to lean in and learn from the wisdom within this book? Let these chapters speak into your heart and life. You can choose to open the pages and let them pour into you, or you can put this book on a shelf. My heart and prayer is that you will say "yes" to you and lean into the powerful messages of hope, wisdom, love inspiration and courage that are waiting to pour into you, your heart, and your life.

Here is how to get the most out of this powerful book. It is divided it into three powerful sections containing dynamic legacy stories. We divided the chapters into three sections that will inspire, encourage and empower you" "**Legacies of Great Courage and Strength**"; "**Legacies of Connection,**

Intention and Purpose"; and "Legacies of Great Love and Joy." I encourage you to pick the section that pulls at your heart and then choose a chapter or two to read. Quick warning.... I believe as you start reading...☺. You may find yourself wanting to keep reading as each powerful chapter touches your heart and life; at the end of each chapter, the contact information and a little bit about each author. I know that they would love to hear from you, to know how their chapter connected with you.

Now the next step is yours. Pour yourself a cup of coffee or tea and drink-in the stories and messages that are within these pages to serve, support, and inspire you. Take the time to pause, read, and reflect. Listen to the powerful messages of hope that are waiting for you within the pages of this book. It's not an accident that you purchased this book and you are opening it to read right now, today. I invite you to lean in and truly receive the messages and wisdom that will speak to your heart and soul. Enjoy this rich collection of wisdom, love, and encouragement. May these legacy stories touch your heart and life…and inspire you to celebrate your legacy stories and even start a legacy of your own.

ABOUT THE COMPILER
Rebecca Hall Gruyter

Founder/Owner of Your Purpose Driven Practice and CEO of RHG Media Productions.

Rebecca Hall Gruyter is an influencer and empowerment leader that wants to help you reach more people. She has built multiple businesses and platforms to help influencers and experts reach more people. Through her conferences, workshops, and live events are designed to quip and empower you to step forward and SHINE. Through her collaborative books (over 15 of them …. most of them best sellers) she seeks to support readers while lifting up her co-authors, experts, and Influencers….to help them reach even more people around the world.

Rebecca's International radio show (Empowering Women, Transforming Lives) is currently played though 10 different networks and 12 different channels. Her international TV Show currently released through 4 different TV Networks features experts and influencers bringing them to a global market place. Her RHG Magazine and TV Guide is shared in over 50 countries. Her TV Network called the RHG TV Network that features over 7 TV Channels each producing and sharing multiple programs and TV Shows around the world! Recently, she received the honor of one of the top 10 working women of America for her empowerment work in the area of entrepreneurship.

Rebecca is the CEO of RHG Media Productions, Founder/Owner of the RHG TV Network, Network Director of the Women's Channel of 'VoiceAmerica' in both TV and radio and the Founder/Owner of Your Purpose Driven Practice and the Creator of the Speaker Talent Search. Rebecca has created a promotional reach of over 7 million and today…. she wants to share with you…. How you too, can be seen and heard on multiple platforms and SHINE!

(925) 787-1572

Rebecca@YourPurposeDrivenPractice.com

www.facebook.com/rhallgruyter (Face book)

www.YourPurposeDrivenPractice.com (Main Website)

www.RHGTVNetwork.com (TV Network)

www.SpeakerTalentSearch.com (Free Opportunity for Speakers to get on More Stages)

www.EmpoweringWomenTransformingLives.com (Weekly Radio Show)

www.MeetWithRebecca.com (Calendar link to schedule a time to talk with Rebecca)

ACKNOWLEDGEMENTS

When writing an anthology, it takes many voices that are willing to join together to bring forth the book in a powerful and united way. It has been such an honor and privilege to work with this amazing group of authors. I want to thank these amazing authors for entrusting us to bring forth and share their treasured legacy stories.

I want to thank my husband for always cheering me on and encouraging me to SHINE! I thank God for giving me opportunities, opening doors, and bringing together the right people for this powerful project. I want to thank my parents for their love and support and my grandmothers for planting the legacy seeds to always choose to Bloom and SHINE!

We thank Women on a Mission Enterprises (WOM) and their powerful team for embracing our vision for this book and helping us share it with the world.

Legacies of Great Courage & Strength

SHIFTING SANDS
By: Renée Sands

You don't get to choose your DNA. You don't get to choose your family; you didn't get to choose your hair, eye or skin color. Some things in life you just have no input on. It took centuries to form the blood that runs through your veins; generation upon generations. And this is a short story about the DNA of the Sands' family.

I want my grandchildren to understand that they are a part of something that did not begin with them. **A significant part of their lives, their meaning and mattering come from our family story.** Somewhere in our family bloodline we had great, great grandparents who prayed diligently for the family blood line. We were and are God fearing, Torah walking and holy spirit believing family of God.

As a grandmother, my life story begins with my mother and fathers having lived 35 years of their lives in Africa. My parents both have Caribbean blood lines, my father from the Bahamas and my mother from Trinidad. They grew up during World War two. **They had to live through the depression which caused them to believe in hard work and I do mean hard work and an education were your only way to financial freedom and the American dream.** I remember my mother telling me how she would sell bottles for 5 cents for bread. **Everyone shared everything.** You had family clothes and family shoes. **Everything was passed down**. Most families lived together or at least nearby. It was understood that you were dependent on others for your existence and helping one another was the way life was.

My father was a quiet man. He did very little talking, and seemed to me to always be in deep thought. He was a man of firsts. He was one of the original Tuskegee, Airman with the Air force 616th Bombardier Squad. He was the first in the family to graduate from college and one of the first black men to graduate from Cornell University with a PHD. Times were tough for him. **He endured racial discrimination that was so painful he never would talk about it.** One story he told me once was when a professor told him 'no matter how good a paper or a project you do, you will only get a C grade because no black man could ever be above a C grade.' As Tuskegee Airmen, they endured belittling, ridiculing, and were treated as inferior human beings.

Despite of all that these men were the only fighting pilots that never lost a plane they were protecting during the war. They became known as the Red Tails and became sought after by their white counterparts when they realized that these men were exceptional pilots. Today in the New African American museums his Tuskegee Airman equipment is on permanent display. **He was a man of great character, physical and mental strength.** A legacy I am proud to honor and share with the world.

My mother is a stunning beautiful woman. She is 97 years old as I write this. You know the saying that behind every great man is an equally, awesome woman, well that was my mother. Her world was my father, me and my brother and sister; as a woman of those times, that was supposed to be everything a woman would need or want. My parents were married for 57 years, before my father died.

The history of how as a family we ended up in Africa for 35 years would at least be a chapter in itself. But what the devil meant for evil the Lord turned out for good. My father was first sent by the AME church to Suacoco Liberia to work the land and show the Liberians how to develop new profitable crops for exportation. While in Liberia he became one of the founders of the Agricultural Department at Cuttington College. We lived in Liberia for 7 years and my brother was born in Suacoco. One of the crops I can remember the farmers frequently grew was coffee. We would have huge 50lb bags of coffee lined up in the hallway before they were exported. **The smell of coffee permeated the house and till this day I love coffee and the smell of it.** It always reminds me of Liberia and that time that we lived there.

Every two to four years we would move to another country. From Liberia, we moved to Ibadan Nigeria, to Enugu, Nigeria, North and South Sudan and on and on it goes. Where ever my parents lived and schooling was not available my brother, sister and I went to boarding schools. Eventually I ended up going to boarding schools in Nigeria,

Egypt, and France. The three of us did not always end up in the same schools. For example, my brother was in Switzerland and my sister went to Israel while I was in France.

I didn't have television or a lot of toys when living in Africa. I was surrounded with wildlife and had pets as my friends. In Enugu, Nigeria we were 500 miles away from the nearest town, truly living in the Jungle. The most we had was a short-wave radio and music from the local villages. I played and went to elementary school in the village. My parents entertained a lot so there was always a feel of excitement and joy around the house and amazing local food. To this day, I carry a love of animals, local food, and entertaining others/connecting with others.

I want my grandchildren to know the history of our family having traveled to over 16 countries and having lived all over the world. We are an international family that has a worldview on life. We are a family that the Holy Spirit kept safe and free from disease all those years living in Africa and traveling the world. We didn't have medical care as you know it now. We have been on thousands of flights, eaten in unsanitary places, drank unpurified water and none of us ever had to be evacuated back to the States. I believe we were kept safe because my parents were living on purpose, for a purpose and doing what God sent them to do on earth.

My parents were a blessing wherever they went and always left the countries we lived in better off than when they first arrived. We can all choose to carry this legacy forward. Choose to be a blessing and leave a place better than when you arrive there. I believe that traveling and living overseas is the best education one can have; a legacy I'm proud of and thankful for. Meeting people from all over the world and being exposed to different cultures gives you an appreciation for the evidence of God. **When you get to see the beauty in others way of life and how much we have in common it is impossible to teach hate.**

Mothers all love their children, fathers protect their family, food and water is needed by everyone, animal lovers are everywhere, we all need air to breathe and we are all fearfully and wonderfully made. **There are no accidental people on earth. You cannot sneak onto earth. We all matter and we all were brought to earth with a purpose.** I want my grandchildren to know that living on purpose, with a purpose and for a purpose is why they are here. We have a responsibility running through our DNA. Our family story is not typical for any family much less a Black family. Their grandparents and great grandparents were men and women of strong character. Many times, they were the first in their family to go to college, own a home or run a business.

They were uncompromising in doing the right thing and treating all human beings with dignity and respect. I encourage and challenge you; our powerful reader to be willing to be the first…pave the way for another. For you to have the courage to do the right thing and treat all human beings with dignity and respect. We are all here on purpose and for a purpose. I want all of us to choose to build a legacy. We are all proud to pass down and share with future generations.

I want my grandchildren to know that they have greatness and power running through their veins. The blood in their bodies is crying out for the light that is in them to shine out. **As the legacy of the Sands' family moves on through them; they are to be a blessing to the world. There is brilliance in each of them that no one else has, a purpose and a plan for each of them that no one else can accomplish for the Sands family, just like I believe this of you and your family.**

They are not to wait for someone to discover them. They are to discover it themselves. Their service to the world will be legendary. They will make their past generations proud. You also can choose to discover yourself and bring forward your gifts, legacies, and choose to leave the world, communities, and positions better than how you found them.

I began by saying that no one gets to choose their family. This Sands' family DNA was chosen for them by an all knowing everlasting God. I cannot wait to see what comes forth from them. Both of my children have become entrepreneurs, starting their own companies taking the path less chosen by the masses.

It has not been easy for them even today they face racial discrimination; but all I have to do at times is remind them of the struggle of their grandparents. And tell them how despite of everything they went through they never gave up. We are to be the lenders and not the borrowers, the givers and not the takers of this world. I'm honored, proud and celebrate that so many of the Sands' family has chosen to bring forward their gifts and contributions and I am excited to see what our children and grandchildren will bring forward.

Powerful reader, what is the legacy you are bringing forward? What are you choosing to do on purpose and with purpose to give to this world and future generations? I would like to share some wisdom I received as I pulled together this chapter and had the privilege of sharing my family legacy. From my heart to yours, here are the gems of wisdom to bringing forth a legacy you can be proud of and celebrate.

Legacy Tips:

1. Be willing to be first
2. Work hard and leave things better than you found them
3. Do the right thing even when it's not popular
4. Share and pass down
5. Be a person of great character & Integrity
6. Connect with others/ your gift is not for you
7. Live on purpose
8. Be a blessing
9. Choose to see the beauty in others
10. Things do not bring happiness.

About the Author

Renée Sands coaches patients, listeners and clients on how to improve their well-being by teaching on the roots of disease. Renée is a certified life coach and Registered Nurse with over 40 years of experience. She delivers simple, straightforward, real-life solutions to deal with issues like stress, bitterness and fear which have medical correlations to cancer, diabetes and hypertension.

Renée is world traveler who grew up in a military lifestyle throughout Europe and Africa. This rich history of cultural exposure affords her a unique world view and insight into people from all walks of life. Her engaging personality led her naturally into nursing, coaching and medical missions. She has been blessed to broadcast, facilitate and partner with the following: Be in Health, the ministry of Pastor Henry Wright; Church in the Son led by Pastor Alex Clattenburg; the Janet Mefferd Show; and Joyce Meyer Ministries Hands of Hope.

As the former radio personality of her own show, *All Things Spiritual*, Renée reached listeners in 120 countries through well-known and respected radio stations, WINB and WTLN. She became a Certified Life Coach under the mentoring of Dr. Michael J. Duckett and recently completed her Certificate in Mind Body Healing from the Wellness Professionals in Health based in the UK. She began *Kingdom Meditation* as a way to equip and educate clients on the spiritual root of disease so they can see positive changes in their lives. Renée is a mother of two and grandmother to three wonderful grandsons.

Social Media Links

Email Address: info@kingdom-meditation.com

Phone Number: 770-715-9914

Website: www.kingdom-meditation.com

Facebook page: https://www.facebook.com/Kingdom-Meditation-462325847279707/

LinkedIn Page:

Twitter handle: https://twitter.com/King_Meditation

YouTube Channel:

Other Social Media Channels:
https://www.instagram.com/kingdom_meditation/

LEGACY OF COURAGE SOARING WITH DRAGONS
By: Victoria C. Leo

Rose was born into and enculturated in a world in which kings were obeyed without question, and duty and honor were the highest strivings of the heart. When the kings chose war, she lived through four years of utter hell, forcing herself to go on in helpless fear, as the casualties in the trenches mounted into the millions. With every day that went by, the likelihood increased that her fiancée would never come home to her, and the life they had planned together, farming in the foothills of the Alps, would never be.

When her PTSD-wracked survivor returned, it was to a year of starvation and despair. As a million of her countrymen and women died of starvation in the cities, Rose in her rural village survived on tree bark, moss, water cress, insects and squirrels. She tried to immigrate to the United States, but quotas were filled for years to come.

Rose and her fiancée didn't stay and fester in resentment like Corporal Hitler and millions of other survivors; instead, they found another country that was actively recruiting farmers. Ultimately, Rose couldn't live with bugs the size of an aircraft carrier clearly, an inherited trait! Grand-dad reluctantly sold his new farm and they embarked on another cross-ocean immigrant voyage, successfully achieving entry to the United States from Brazil. Arriving with no resources, relatives, friends or English, they studied language furiously, found work as servants and eventually bought cheap real estate which they turned into a boarding house for Rose to run.

Lily traveled on an immigrant ship alone, to an arranged marriage with a man two decades her senior. Her husband loved being a musician and didn't really want the responsibilities of family life, but being a happy single guy wasn't an option in his immigrant culture. A teenaged new wife with limited English, she quickly made friends in the language and community she understood, and started her lifelong quest to perfect, accent-free English fluency.

Four decades later, when her husband had died and her son was launched on his own parenting trajectory, Rose poured her powerful intellect and business drive into a successful real estate career. The last words she spoke on this Earth were instructions to my aunt concerning one of her properties: a tenant had a leak that needed fixing.

For both my grandmothers, the female burden of reproduction and society's definitions of gender played major roles. Rose chose two illegal and unsafe pregnancy terminations while she and grand-dad were servants, because they would both have lost their livelihoods if she had continued a pregnancy. For a devout Catholic couple, this was yet another trauma for them to overcome. When they bought the boarding house, Grandma Rose could finally start a family in her forties.

Lily had the opposite sadness: after a son was born, she lost several pregnancies. In keeping with the times, since these failed pregnancies were threatening her life, her doctor advised her to begin artificial birth control or embrace abstinence.

Granddad feared community censure if he bucked the prevailing Catholic doctrine against birth control, so her sex life ended in her late twenties. Mother to only one child in a culture where a woman's status and stature in the community existed in proportion to the size of her living brood was not an enviable position. Lily attempted adoption but rules involving lower-middle income immigrants were strict and she was turned down. She mourned her lost children, quietly, in her heart, to the end of her days.

Their lives are eerily similar to mine, in that I barely survived an ectopic pregnancy. **The politics of power through reproduction has changed in a century, but the pain of lost children is a universal that echoes through my biological lineage and that of all living women, everywhere in the world.**

The ravages and trauma of World War I on Rose and her cohort, impacted her children as well. Her own courage and resiliency did not manifest in the next generation; one of her daughters (my birth mother) was a deeply abusive parent, partly as a result of sexist society's thwarting of her career dreams, but also I believe as a result of pain absorbed from the trauma of her mother's generation. Rose survived incredible horrors, but she did not survive unscathed, and either through epigenetics or through her upbringing, my birth mother carried that pain into another generation. Parents of that generation had no skilled professional support for their healing journey and, sadly, coping solely on your own has limits.

Grandma Rose's failure as a parent fills me with compassion, and I firmly believe that if your survival makes you fearful and always expecting additional troubles, you're not weak or less-brave than the people who move through their trouble with less long-term impact. You can develop wisdom from suffering, and that is the narrative that we all want to hear, but sometimes we forget to be compassionate with the human beings who are failing to fulfill our desired script. The suffering that I endured through my childhood is, in a very real sense, the end of the arc that started with the starvation and terror of World War I, as Rose and her husband did the best they could with their war-seared, and obedience-oriented, psyches, and no professional support.

Barely a decade after they were able to start their family, their new country was once again at war with their former country. Their fears for their families must have been a daily searing agony as the arc of the war turned toward massive bombing of German cities. The official story from grand-dad was always one of clear, unambiguous American patriotism, but, after all, I do have a Masters degree in Psychology. The man who was raised in the Kaiser's world of uncomplicated devotion to country spoke what he wanted to be true, what an honorable man would want to be true, but I know the true workings of the human heart.

I remember Jeanne Houston's words in **Farewell to Manzanar**, concerning immigrant Japanese Americans in the same war: "When your mother and your father are having a fight, do you want them to kill each other? Or do you just want them to stop fighting?"

Eventually the two countries did stop fighting, but the war and immediate post-war years were filled with days of constant suspicion and ostracism. Though not equivalent to being herded into barbed-wire camps and stripped of homes, farms and resources, it was another emotionally fraught experience in their lifetime of traumas.

One legacy of my two amazing grandmothers is my Middle Atlantic accent, a tribute to where their immigrant journeys ended, where they dug deep roots into a new land and created a new identity, where their children met and married and where I was born and spent my early years. Both of them poured their love into me in the form of incredible, traditional European food, spiced and cooked with precision and intuitive flair. **Their most important legacy, of course, is their courage.**

My own life trajectory has included several very serious health challenges, including a thirty year significant pain condition. My resume (CV) is quite impressive but, **like Rose, I battled hard to survive and thrive. Like her, I've done what I needed to do to survive, and survive honorably.** When I could not afford college tuition and rent, I chose college and was homeless for almost two of my 3.5 years, cleverly using college gym facilities to maintain neatness and cleanliness.

I collected leftover food from the college cafeteria to supplement the food I bought, with my minimum-wage job. I slept where I could - on couches in various friends' homes, on the library floor, in the college steam tunnels in the depths of winter and under bushes in quiet, upscale neighborhoods in summer. I figured that dogs in upscale neighborhoods were unlikely to have rabies, and I was right. My undergrad journey horrifies some people, because they don't know the details of what Rose survived. **I was on fire to get the education that would save me from a lifetime of poverty, the same passion to succeed and thrive that drove Rose and Lily.**

Yet, until three years ago, I had completely closed off all thoughts of my biological ancestry and all the rich inspiration that it could have provided me. **All my attention focused on my adoptive family, who rescued me from Rose and Lily's children and gave me the love, the hope and the belief in my essential goodness that allowed my soul to soar and my heart to heal.** It took a mountain of effort to release the results of my childhood abuse, but I accomplished it, soaring into a lifetime of achievement, and, two decades ago, a career in transformation and healing.

Using clinical hypnotherapy, life coaching, master-level Reiki energy healing and other tools, I crafted individual transformation programs to blast away blockages in my female professionals' complicated lives.

My work has given thousands of people healthy, vibrant futures, including survivors of PTSD derived from violence, war, traffic accidents and other traumas. I've also had a transformative impact on many entrepreneurs who need encouragement and concrete how-to's to effectively conquer the stress that is killing their bodies and blunting their income and success.

My heart thrills with each of them as they soar into a new life trajectory for not only themselves, but their children as well. In every one, I see an echo of Grandmothers Lily and Rose, who had to navigate their lives without skilled help. It is the 21st Century now, skilled help is available and I am providing it.

Yet, I was soaring with only one wing. The wing of my biological ancestry was still broken. It was as if I were living in a box with only one exit. I took the exit, but there was a whole rich and wonderful world beyond the 2nd blocked-up exit that I could not see and could not access.

One day, while taking an intensive guided journey, just like the ones I do for my clients, I had a vision. The resulting webinar, **Meet Your Ancestors**, takes you on a journey of 10,000 generations to meet and learn from all those ancestors. Attendees find it transformational. It certainly was for me, because I not only connected with all those thousands of remote generations, I connected with my grandparents as well. In a warm rush, I could feel all of Rose and Lily's courage and resiliency, resourcefulness and refusal to be defeated, activating inside of me. **(https://www.learnitlive.com/class/9895/Meet-Your-Biological-Ancestors)**

Connecting with my four grandparents was more profound than words can convey. Perhaps it is the blasting through of that 2nd exit from the box. Now, I fly with two wings flapping. Now, when I soar, I am truly a soaring dragon. As Supreme Court Justice Sonia Sotomayor so eloquently puts it in her autobiography: "People who live in difficult circumstances need to know that there are happy endings."

On the 100th anniversary of the Great War that devastated Rose's world and sent her on two major trans-oceanic migrations, her descendant is freeing trauma survivors like her from the mental prison that she could not escape. I plant her life like a flag on my healing work, and on my life. Grandmother Rose's voyages into the future continue through me and every life that I have altered, and all the happy and successful generations that will follow.

In our century, the effects of trauma aren't eternal. Courage, however, still is.

'Trauma' doesn't just mean childhood abuse, war or surviving a violent crime. It also means traffic accidents, bad breakups or divorces, and harsh or unfair outcomes in your career. If you own a business and lost an opportunity for any reason other than your competence, you've experienced the betrayal of your belief in meritocracy. All these events leave traces deep in your unconscious mind.

Do you have a business, but aren't getting clients because you don't have the cool, break-out ideas that clients need? Do you want to start a business or write a novel, but it's just not happening? Are you 'stuck'?

The good news is that you CAN get the break-out ideas, and you CAN get unstuck, permanently and forever. The first step to your permanent transformation is my **5 Tools in 5 Minutes/Day** program, **yours absolutely free**. *Do this program for 30 days – just 5 minutes/day – and see yourself shift from stuck to inspired, as you transform yourself at a deep and permanent level.*

This special program is distilled from my book **101 Stress Busters for Energy, Joy & Healthy Longevity**, focusing on the 5 tools with the absolutely highest ROI (return on investment) of your time and effort.

What is keeping you from the break-out business ideas and the courage and inspiration to tackle your other dreams and goals is a seemingly mighty boulder in your path? What Hannibal of Carthage did when a big rock blocked his army's path through the Alps seems so simple?

He heated the rock and then poured acid on it and it cracked into a dozen smaller pieces that his men could easily shove down the mountainside. The road through the tallest mountains in Europe was open!

Your commitment to go deep, to the source of the boulder in your deep unconscious, is the fire. These five tools are the acidic vinegar. A common substance, wielded in the right way, with the right conditions, can be more powerful than solid rock.

Commit to these 5 tools for 5 Minutes, for at least 30 days, and watch your life transform! Joy, ease and a powerful feeling of "rightness" about your life is your birthright as a human being. You can do it, and I am right here by your side all the way!

https://blastthruthosebarriers.thinkific.com/courses/106742

My book **101 Stress Busters for Energy, Joy & Healthy Longevity** (https://www.amazon.com/101-Stress-Busters-More-Meditation/dp/1541311833/) will complement your 30 day test drive with over 86 FUN activities that have a measureable positive impact on your physical health, energy and joy.

Need a 30-second kick-start? https://youtu.be/wYAmJyOfsMw

You can fly powerfully, with both your wings, to a glorious new future. Make the commitment. You, my dear dragons, will never fly alone. I will always be flapping at your side, over the mountains, through the valleys and over the wide oceans that Rose and Lily crossed.

About the Author

Victoria Leo focuses on you - professionals 35+ years old, who have kids, cats, parents, poodles, bills and battling insurance companies. She will teach you how to get the income you want through breakout ideas – the same stress-busting road that will give you the energy, vitality and longevity that is your genuine, heartfelt desire.

With her no-nonsense, bottom-line approach married to genuine warmth and caring, her proven programs will blast you past the mental and practical barriers that have been holding you back from living the life you deserve to have, from creative stress-busting for entrepreneurs and professionals, all the way to trauma-healing for PTSD. Thousands of women like you have been given new life trajectories through these in-depth custom programs, and through her online classes. Victoria wrote her first published book in 1985 for Prentice-Hall. Recent titles, focused on her clients' most urgent needs, include **101 Stress Busters for Energy, Joy and Healthy Longevity** (2017), **101 Healthy Meals in 5 Minutes** or Less, **2nd Ed** (2017) and **Journey Out of SAD: Beat the Seasonal Blues Now, 2nd Ed.** (2016), available in print and e-book formats.

Victoria@soaringdragon.biz
253-653-5995
www.soaringdragon.biz

https://www.facebook.com/Soaring-Dragon-295337430525356/
www.linkedin.com/in/victoriacleo
www.youtube.com/user/humanbio4everyone/videos
https://www.pinterest.com/victorialeoreik/
http://soaringdragoninjapan.blogspot.com/
Online classes!
https://blastthruthosebarriers.thinkific.com/courses/106742

LIVE WITHOUT RESERVATIONS
By: Colleen Sandra Quinn

I am basking in the glorious, golden glow of the sun, so sweet after the depressing dreariness of a drab, drawn out winter. The air is crisp, clear, exhilarating - made intoxicating from the exalted fragrance wafting through the air from the blossom-laden row of country lilacs lining the yard. Oh, it feels so good to be outside, I am giddy with glee. I turn hearing the stretched spring squeak as the porch screen door opens and then slams shut as Nana, hair rolled up and back, eyelet apron over a flowered print house dress, strides towards me, her eyes shining bright as our eyes connect in a shared knowing. She reaches her arm up high to pull down a bountiful bough and we both deeply inhale with passionate exuberance. She hums, it is her soothing and soulful two note melody as she lets go of the branch, and wraps her arms around me with a great loving hug from behind. **In this moment, I am safe, I am home, I belong, I am loved** – time stands still and opens into a vast expansive space of wonder, and possibility in a way that words cannot dutifully express.

This memory etched vividly on my heart was made more poignant with Nana's passing in the fall of that year, when I was eight, shortly after our family moved from Prince Edward Island to the fruit and garden filled Niagara region in Ontario. My young heart ached but I did not really understand why or what to do with the feeling of emptiness. Over the years I often sought out stories of grandmothers holding my cup to that deep well I had drank from that left a thirst for more. Recently, when participating in a meditation with Grandmother Flordemayo, one of the Council of Thirteen Grandmothers, she began to hum and I smiled as I relaxed into receiving the 'joyful noise' and was carried home to myself, my Nana. Humming, which my mother did as well, if you are open to it creates the feeling of being cradled in the arms of love, cherished really –a beautiful experience.

The older I become the more meaning continues to emerge and unfold from my beyond time heart connection with Nana. When I was younger, I thought my memory was about a shared love of lilacs, for the sight or smell of them forever evokes home to me. Every place I have lived, I have planted one or more lilac trees to ceremoniously anoint the house to be a home, and in loving memory of Nana. Do you have a ritual you use to make your house a home? Many of Nana's favourite flowers are treasured friends in my garden- the wild tiger lilies, peonies, dahlias, morning glories, and hollyhocks. My home is my sanctuary, my space for curiosity and creativity that nurtures my resilience so I can successfully navigate through the inevitable ups, downs and the ways of life. **My grandmother taught me the strength in facing things head on.**

When my brother was a young boy there was a man whose face was contorted, he spoke with a slur and walked with a limp. "I am afraid of him" he told my grandmother, and the next time the man passed her home she invited him in for tea and suggested my brother join them. My brother was amazed to discover this man was gentle, bright and funny and within that alchemical meeting, the fear was transformed into the planted seed of compassion.

Nana was patient and loving. When all thirteen of her children had diphtheria at the same time she lovingly nursed them all back to health. She understood the power, the love, the difficulties and the joy that came with motherhood. In the fullness of time, my remembrance of Nana has evolved to see the compassion, the connection with nature, the land, the ocean, and our ancestors something my grandmother taught me without ever speaking about it. **Nana's most profound wisdom teachings were always through her actions.**

I believe within that stride out to me was a confidence, a self-love, a carried wisdom of living life in the present moment – before it had become a popular declaration to do so. Those bright shining eyes held a depth of compassion where even in the most challenging personal times she found something to share with someone with needs greater than her own, whether it be the warmth of a fire, food, clothing, a hug or words of comfort. My mother will tell you there was also fierceness, a tough love quality.

I have seen and felt this up close with one of my most beloved teachers, Marion Woodman. Once in a private moment, Marion looked me directly in the eye when I was feeling vulnerable and unsure of making the big changes my heart carried, declaring I must do what it takes to let the child in me dance free, she was fierce, would not accept excuses and invoked a strength in me, and her eyes had a youthful sparkle that belied her age. In Marion's eyes, I felt Nana's bright eyes mirrored back encouraging me and lighting my path forward.

Once after a family Thanksgiving dinner my brother revealed that Nana was born on the M'ikmaq Lennox Island reservation in PEI.

It wasn't so much a family secret as a surprising error of omission. Here I was in my forties and yet something awakened in me and I immediately knew myself better, as if a puzzle piece I did not realize was missing gently fell into place. After that I became more aware of Nana's presence, especially when making decisions to follow my heart.

She was there supporting me in my decision to leave a confining relationship I had long outgrown; she smiled with joy when in my fifties I pursued my Master's degree in Depth Psychology; she filled me with strength and love as my husband went through a series of health challenges. She stood steadfast in helping me hear my inner 'YES' when I left the corporate world to establish my own company to be a transformational change strategist, advocate and coach. My coaching has always been about truth telling, nurturing the authentic full expression of gifts and helping clients hear and then take the next step calling to them.

In her first marriage, my grandmother found she was with a stingy, big ego of a man who seemed to work hard to keep her joy of life constrained, reigned in. He railed against any independence and threatened to leave her declaring she would end up destitute living in a shack. She was industrious and resourceful in the kinds of jobs she would do, such as laundry, to help provide for the family and others. She always had an elegant and powerful presence. My mother remembers when Nana covered a wagon with freshly pressed linen, and placed just picked, plump, bursting with flavor blueberries in shimmering large crystal bowls with real whipped cream contained on ice and took to the streets and earned money.

Hers was a quiet, inner power that gave her the strength of character to pursue a divorce in the 1930's, one of the first on Prince Edward Island. Any talk of divorce at that time, came with scandal, gossip and outright rejection, and yet she persevered and obtained the formal passing of an Act of Canadian Parliament required in those times to receive a divorce. I marvel at her brave heart and how at mid-life she chose not to resign herself to a life of quiet misery and instead chose to allow for more love, more joy, more freedom, more living.

Clearly a woman ahead of her times, out in front as a way-shower for others. I invite you to pause and reflect on the courage that must have taken. I think of all the support systems that are available to us now and yet she boldly stepped forward alone, supported only by her determination and the faith in her heart. I can feel her right now ushering me into new and expanded expressions of myself. Is there an action your heart is calling you to take on your journey of becoming? My Nana wants us to know you and I have the courage to act on our heart's desires.

In her second marriage, she found true love and enjoyed more abundance, always continuing to share and open her home and dining room to those who needed it. In this more prosperous time her elegance was highlighted with clothes as she had flair in the wearing of an outfit or a hat; **but it was never the clothes that carried this sense of style as it was her essence, her presence, the comfort in her own skin.**

I am struck by the fact that while she was born on a reservation she lived her life without reservation. By that, I do not mean she turned her back on her reservation for she embodied the M'ikmaq culture of compassion, sharing, resourcefulness in surviving and always finding a way through to find peace and harmony. Providing food and the sharing of food was a great act of love and joy to my Nana, as it was with my mother and now her children along with many treasured traditions. **Sunday at Nana's was always open house and whoever showed up would be welcomed and fed with compassion, dignity and respect.**

It feels as if she had a connection and wisdom in her ways that was beyond her, a story carrier in the tradition of her ancestors. She lived without reservation by not getting entangled, tied down and held back by stereotypes, labels, myths, the ego or the thinking of the small mind, she transcended it all and in that kitchen wisdom way she would chide or nudge people to get over themselves if they were letting their pride to become overly worked up over something. **For Nana, it was not about a striving over, it was always about a move to live life fully allowing access to more love, peace and harmony.**

Annie Jane Frances, my Nana, was born in 1881, often having a tough, hard life growing up on the reservation surviving the harshest of nature's elements living on the wild, rugged and red soil shores of the Atlantic Ocean. My mother, the youngest of Nana's children, remembers quietly going off to the reservation with her mother on Saturdays as a young girl. I so wish I could have joined them, experiencing the daily life, traditions, the pow-wows, ceremonies, stories and community. My mother says it was clear Nana was in her element, her joy, when they were at the reservation. I wonder if Nana sometimes felt alone in her beliefs and ways.

I believe her knowing eyes knew I would play a role in carrying the story forward as the door does not close, the story continues to unfold. I regularly speak with Nana in my meditations and journal writing and of course I hum, often feeling she is humming right along with me. I am inspired by my Nana and this continues to have deep meaning for me with each passing day. As I enter elder hood, Nana is helping me, hand firmly at my back, to expand into this new life phase, guiding me to be more contemplative, to deepen my spirituality and daily practices as a preparation to embrace what is coming next, to let go of my definitions and allow for something new to emerge, a new way of being. In the paradox of life, I who loves the grandmother role do not have children and am not a grandmother in the traditional sense.

I can however be a Grand Mother in embracing and valuing all of humanity and as Gandhi said "to be the change in the world I want to see" and allow my own compassion to inspire others.

I was born after my mother had lost a little boy, Michael, at birth. In those days, you were expected to just get over it and move on. My sister remembers seeing a little newborn's sailor suit wrapped in tissue paper tucked away in a drawer ready for the homecoming. It must have been difficult for my mum to open her heart to another child while still grieving the loss of her little boy. My mother has always loved me, I know that, but I feel it is my Nana that has given me my true sense of belonging and purpose. Now in my sixties, I appreciate the truth Nana carried in how she lived her life. I feel the best way to honor Nana, is to embrace my own opportunity to be a way shower and to continue to discover and reveal more of my own brave and courageous heart.

In these times of amazing access and acquiring of information at our fingertips, it is easy to confuse knowledge with wisdom. I believe we all at some level deeply yearn for the wisdom of our elders from their life experiences, a wisdom that is deeply needed as a generational love that continues to be passed on and gives us a tangible felt sense of something we can trust and rings true in our hearts.

I hope you can feel within my Nana's story, my story, and in fact all of our stories. **I believe we can choose to carry the strengths of our ancestors forward in creating both our own life and a caring for the life of future generations.** It is our heritage and why I am committed to carry my grandmother's strengths and some of my own as I continue to live our unfolding story **and so I ask you to listen deeply to your own heart now – Are you living your life without reservation?** What brave and courageous step is your heart asking you to take next? What story are you carrying?

Where can you get over yourself? All of those 'yes, buts' and rationalizations, what is keeping you from listening to your own compassionate heart? Is your pride keeping resentment, fear or judgment alive in you?

Are you allowing your heart to open, to expand? Right now in this very moment what can you open to trust, to receive, to allow more of in your life that will bring more peace, more joy, more harmony, more love?

How can you extend your maternal, or paternal nurturing for a child, all of our children, our future generations?
Have you fully expressed your Grand Mother?
What is the teaching wisdom carried in your own actions?
What strengths from your grandmother can you choose to carry forward?

If you are ever feeling lost, try humming and I promise you will be carried by the sacred sound back to your truth, your still point; And above all, Always Allow For Love.

About the Author

Colleen is a passionate coach and change advocate with a roster of clients across North America. She is valued as an intuitive, strategic thinker and trusted advisor. Since she was a teenager, she has been sought out as an inspirational guide assisting others to claim their true gifts, by listening and answering the call of the heart. She is passionate that everyone experiences the freedom and joy in living their truth and expressing their full creative power. Over the past six years her coaching has also included entrepreneurs looking to identify their niche or grow their current business. Her organizational change management experience has been focused in the financial, technology, energy and telecommunication sectors.

Colleen holds a BA from University of Waterloo, and her MA is from Pacifica Graduate Institute (CA). She enjoys writing, gardening, learning to play the harp and hiking near her cabin in the woods in Northern Ontario's Algonquin Park. She lives with her family in the Niagara region, Ontario, Canada.

callings@rogers.com
289.219.4433
shiftconsultinc.com
www.facebook.com/colleen.quinn.5492
www.linkedin.com/in/colleen-quinn-b0491410
shiftconsultinc@ShifttoShine

CONNECTION AND CELEBRATION
By: Catherine M. Laub

Momoo is my maternal grandmother and she lived on a farm upstate New York. We visited often and I have a special feeling when I think about visiting.

When I was about 10 years old I told Momoo that nobody ever calls me Catherine. She decided from that moment forward she will call me Catherine while everyone else kept calling me Cathy. This reminder helped me decide on what name I wanted to use professionally. I can hear her calling me Catherine and feeling special because of it.

One of my favorite memories is the cookie hole stand. When we had cookies with holes, we put the "holes" on the stick. Momoo had a special stand that my grandfather made to put our 'holes' on. It looked similar to the toy where the bottom is larger than the top and different sized rings get stacked on. We would eat the round cookie and when it was finished we saved the "hole" to put onto this stand. We knew it was imaginary but loved the connection it gave me with Momoo! She would stand in the kitchen or outside and hold the stand and all of us kids lined up to put our "holes" on the stand. I remember the feeling of excitement that this routine gave me because I felt an extra special bond to Momoo!

The best times were spent at night until about 2 am with Momoo, GeeGee (my mother), and other various relatives. We played Yahtzee and other games and had lots of fun. I only realized recently that this may be a reason I have a night clock for being awake and waking late in the morning. This became a tradition for all of the family. We all love to get together and play all sorts of games. We also worked on jigsaw puzzles together.

Momoo had a collection of unique and fun gadgets. We love Momoo's little gadgets that often entertained us. Since they had a farm with cows, there was the wind-up 10-inch realistic cow that walked and wiggled around while it mooed. Then there was the drinking bird that dipped his head into a glass of water and 'drank' it. When he was full he stood up. Just recently I saw one of those birds on a TV show and the man in the show was just as excited to see it as I was. Then there was the sugar spoon with a hole almost as big as the spoon itself. Although we visited about twice a year; almost every time, one of us was still fooled by it when the sugar fell right through the hole. We all looked forward to hearing the cuckoo clock that was in the dining room. Now when I hear a cuckoo clock I think about Momoo and her wonderful sense of humor, love, and joy of the unique and the unusual.

Momoo kept a crib up at all times because there was always some family member who was bringing their baby to visit. In the crib were these hand puppet dolls and a Curious George doll. She kept coloring books and crayons, toy cars and dolls for all to play with.

I can picture Momoo in her large vegetable garden wearing her large brimmed hat and gloves, holding her garden tools. My favorite vegetables were her corn and squash. She grew enough each year to cook and freeze to last until the next season. Whenever I eat frozen corn I can remember the taste of Momoo's home grown corn. I remember walking into the woods in the mountains and picking currant berries with Momoo. She made jelly out of them and they were canned to also last the year. The time spent doing these things together gave me a feeling of love and acceptance because I felt lonely at times and like I was the outsider amongst my 5 siblings. Looking back, I now believe Momoo made sure she included me wherever she could so I would know I am appreciated.

I have warm feelings when I think of Momoo. To this day, I know she is one of my spirit guides, and still feel her presence and support throughout my daily life. My first spirit visit through meditation was 5 relatives and she was one of them. They wanted me to know I am on the right path. About 6 months ago I was getting a psychic reading and was told your grandmother is here and she is telling you to slow down. Things will fall into place. I followed that advice and am happy to say things really *are* falling into place.

It's funny, whenever we would talk about visiting my grandparents we didn't say their names, we always said we are going upstate. I felt excitement when we went "upstate" because the surrounding property was a place of wonder. Momoo and Popop allowed us to wander and get fresh air while we played. We would pack our red rubber boots so we could walk on some of the 100 acres to find the cows and bring them home.

There wasn't any garbage collection so she burned everything in a 55-gallon metal container. Along with my grandfather, they had to go in the basement twice daily to tend to the coal stove. That is what heated the very large house. I remember the sheets were always perfectly fitting on the beds. I learned years later that

Momoo always ironed them. That sounded silly to me when I heard it.

All my siblings and cousins have a special place in our hearts for 'the house' which connected all of us during upstate vacations. We had a very large cousin's reunion and all had the opportunity to visit 'the house' and see the changes made by the new owners. We walked around the barn, saw where the hay used to be and the stanchions that held the cows when they weren't out to pasture. This brought back wonderful memories because we played in the hay which was stored upstairs in the barn. The stanchions represented order because each cow knew which one they were assigned to.

Thinking back, I feel Momoo instilled a sense of organization which I don't believe I had at home. To this day I am very unorganized and these memories are helping me put into perspective some of the simple things I can do to get organized. Looking out the window upstairs in the barn we could see the old house where Momoo and Popop lived. They often had wonderful gatherings of numerous family members and I played my violin and others played their instruments while everyone sang together. Momoo always made sure we were happy

My memory in general isn't good so I can't recall if Momoo hugged me or my siblings. I do know she loved us and made sure we were cared for appropriately when we visited. There were always full cooked meals and I remember the closets full of cereal. There was always a choice of what we could eat with the fresh cow's milk.

I mention being hugged because it is something I never learned growing up. I never even saw my parents hug each other. Because of this I didn't hug my children until they were much older and I saw my step-daughters always hugging their children. Now I am always hugging all of my grandchildren. I feel a closer bond than I did with my own mother as I grew up as I carry Momoo's legacy of love and hugging forward.

GeeGee (my grandson named my mother this, but my children call her grandma) has 13 grandchildren and 6 great grandchildren and has always kept up with their adventures, jobs, relationships, etc.

Her legacy is a little different than Momoo's. Most of her grandchildren live locally to her. Most holidays were spent together with my parents, all my siblings, and our children. Once our children began having their own families the holidays became scattered. GeeGee always made sure they all had gifts and enjoyed watching them be opened. Up until recently we all had birthday parties and GeeGee would help every time. Now this legacy of connection and celebration has been passed down to my children and their cousins.

GeeGee has a great sense of humor and all her grandchildren look forward to what funny thing she will say or do next. Although she now has a blood cancer, she has always been very strong and they all know they can count on her to be supportive when they are down. The grandchildren and great-grandchildren love receiving hugs from GeeGee! My son, Richie, told GeeGee never to get rid of her house phone because it's the only phone number he ever memorized. He joked and said "If I'm ever arrested I would be able to call you." LOL

I am Gama (my grandson's name for me) and I love to hug my grandchildren!! I regret not knowing how to show my love to my own children, but they all say it is ok. I didn't grow up being hugged so I didn't learn to hug my children. My belief is that the new generations have a different outlook on raising children. We used to hear the phrase "Children are to be seen, not heard." I believe society in general has evolved in regards to how we show our love to our children and grandchildren. My children spend more time with their children and they are growing up happy and carefree.

I don't remember my paternal grandmother, only from pictures. I do know she is also one of my spirit guides. My father always told me she loved me very much and passed away the day after my first birthday. She was very ill in the hospital and wanted my grandfather to buy me a red dress for my birthday. Once she saw the dress she allowed herself to pass. About eight years ago my father told me he had something for me. He opened his wallet and gave me a mass card from her funeral, which now would be 58 years ago. The card was worn down but I took it with honor and still carry it with me today. Daddy said if I never need any help just to talk to her because she is listening to me.

I pass on to my grandchildren the legacy of knowing I am always available to talk to let them know that they matter and to know there is always something for them to do when they visit us. As my grandmother and mother did, so do I keep coloring books and crayons, toy cars and dolls for them to play with. I have many games for anyone to play with and jigsaw puzzles to be built. There is always time for connection and fun…in fact I plan on it and for it; being prepared for fun just as my grandmother before me did.

Although I have great memories of Momoo and some of her legacies carried down, I believe my own grandchildren have more memories because of living close by and being able to spend more time with us.

My tip for all grandmothers is to listen to your grandchildren. Sometimes they will share something with you that they forgot or won't share with their parents. You may get information that is important for their parents to hear so they can make important changes in their child's life. Be sure to always hug them because they love getting hugs and attention from us. Plan to connect and celebrate…enjoy each other deeply and richly.

My tip to our grandchildren. As you grow older and create your own lives remember that your grandparents are still there for you and want to be included in your life. Share everything with us because we are proud of you and our love is never-ending.

About the Author

Catherine M Laub is a Radio Show Host Author, Speaker, Psychic Medium, and a Spiritual Guide & Consultant; a Wife, Mother, and Grandmother. She is a 9-time bestselling author and continues her writing in upcoming anthologies. These stories are about her healing and spiritual journeys.

Catherine speaks about mental illness in her campaign 'Brighten Your Day with Turquoise,' where she shares her own journey with mental illness and a suicide attempt. Here she guides others to feel invigorated and empowered to go forward in their own struggles. She believes you can do almost anything if you put your mind to it. Catherine's message is that you are not alone and there is a support system waiting for you. Spiritual Destinations is Catherine's radio podcast brought to you by both the Daily Success Network and RHGTV Network. She interviews people about their spirituality and business ventures. Discussions are not limited to spirituality, because Catherine loves to help others and shares modalities to guide them to feeling better.

Catherine psychically delivers information to people from the spiritual realm, their guides and angels that benefit them greatly with their lives. She compassionately guides them to decipher their lives and plan their destinies. Catherine is a workshop facilitator and does readings at local events, as well as performing sessions with clients world-wide.

Her favorite pastimes are making jigsaw puzzles and playing bingo with her mother at local bingo halls. Whenever she gets the chance she travels for vacation and business. The rest of her time is spent with her husband Tony, 7 children and 15 grandchildren. Joshua is her closest because he loves to visit and play with Gama.

catherine@catherinemlaub.com
631-619-2040
www.catherinemlaub.com
https://www.facebook.com/catherine.laub.54
https://www.facebook.com/CatherinesCelestialSpoon
https://www.linkedin.com/in/catherinemlaub
https://twitter.com/cathysquests

HONORING MY FEMININE ROOTS
By: Danielle Nistor

I feel deep down in my heart that this story wants to be written and then be told again and again. This is a story about my grandmothers' lives, their hopes, their gifts and their legacy to the world.

The setting of my story is in rural Romania, a world that was always in a transition going through wars and their devastation, going through communism with its impossible rules of equality that ended the era of constitutional monarchy and disrupted the whole Romanian society especially the people living in the country side by taking away their land and their hopes, and uprooting their customs and traditions.

I thought which one of my grandmothers to choose as the heroine of this story asking my mother and my aunt about those times, and soon I realized that to choose just one of them would not be fair so that this is about both of them.

As a bonus with a healing reflection on my life I will talk here about a third person, the mother of my grandfather from my mother's side who coincidentally or purposefully died exactly the day that I was born. Her name was Stanca and her story is a story of independence, of wisdom and resourcefulness and of strength in the face of adversity.

My grand-grandmother was born a country girl and married a country boy from a village close by as it was customary at that time. After less than 10 years of marriage she was to become a widow with two children as my grand-grandfather never returned from the war. His body was never found and she never had the solace of his grave to go to and live her sorrow. Instead, Stanca would weep her loss every night trying not to disturb her small children.

She was also not able to receive peace of mind by completing the rich burial rituals of the region in which the body of the deceased was dressed with love with the best clothes prepared specifically for this occasion, guarded for two days and nights by people in his home, honored through shared stories about his life, celebrated in a big gathering in the community with lots of food that he loved in his lifetime. The trip to the church and the cemetery was rich with specific customs like: throwing money at the crossroads so that the soul will use it to cross the border of heaven, chants performed by all attending, and other meaningful customs.

A strong belief was that if a soul was not laid to rest in peace it would will come back to haunt the relatives of the deceased. Even though she could not properly burry her husband, Stanca decided not to be overcome by sorrow and fear, and she became the head of the household taking care of the children, the land and the crops. She had no formal education, but she was a beautiful woman and came from a rich family. Soon she became the best tradeswoman well known in the region and the stories that I have heard were that she would trade anything from living animals to fur, wheat, gold and, even diamonds.

She was also a great cook: my aunt still talks about Stanca's baked bread and her pies that were the best in the whole village, and my older sister still remembers her fried cheese dish. She would cook every day for the whole household and also for the workers she employed to work her land. On Fridays, she would carefully prepare eggs, milk and cheese to sell, and early Saturday morning she would get her horse carriage and travel to town, 20 miles away to her faithful lady customers to sell her goods.

Stanca was an open-minded woman and learned quickly from the city women the new customs of the time, bringing home to her family, and selling to other village's delicacies such as: Turkish coffee, Indian tea and Greek halva and olives. Although she never remarried she spent 20 years in a domestic partnership with a German engineer who ended up in the village and fell in love with her.

Stanca died at the age of 87 in her home. I believe that she had fulfilled her life purpose and gracefully allowed herself to transition beyond. She left behind a big homestead with a summer house, a winter house, a guest house, stables and land, and a smiling picture next to my grand-grandfather both young, and dressed in national folk costume.

I often think of her life, her power and her destiny and the connection between the two of us: one living this life as the other was coming into this world. I do invite her sense of power and purpose to bless me, and support me in living my life with gentleness and pride just as she did.

Ralita is my grandmother on my mother's side. She was a tall, beautiful woman, thin, with long dark hair and dark profound eyes. She was quiet and modest, coming from a family that was not as rich as that of my grandfather's John, but who loved her just as much. I am not sure of her dowry but my aunt says she had a few good dresses of lace and of velvet, good shoes, and a long necklace strung of gold coins.

From what I learned about her though, I believe her true dowry was her kind soul and the gift of her hands. She was skilled in everything that has to do with employing her hands; knitting, sewing, weaving and anything else.

In the summer time, she was mostly busy with supervising the workers in the fields, taking care of the garden and the home, but in the winter time she would put the weaving loom in the middle of the room and by spring time she would weave a few carpets; she would also knit many socks, mittens and hats for the children and skillfully sew delicate folkloric patterns on the clothes she made.

After the communism confiscated all their lands, my grandfather was smart enough to start a new business as a beekeeper and Ralita would help him in this endeavor, and also in selling honey in the market. They moved to the city and her life became more comfortable but also estranged as it often happens with people from the country that are used to living in open spaces, where they can connect with nature.

The modern amenities of the city life were also ill fated for her as she was found dead in the bathtub killed by a gas leak when she was only 57 years old. As children, we were not told for few months at the time that she had died and we did not have the chance to say good bye because my parents were afraid of shocking us.

To this day she is to me a woman of love and mystery, and I wish so much to ever find out how she truly felt in her heart behind her serious and sad smile. I sometimes see sparks of her in my aunt

Mary who is ambidextrous as Ralita was and in my sister Michele who resembles her in her beauty, and quiet personality.

Elisabeth is my other grandmother on my father's side and she is also kind of a mystery woman to me. A beautiful young girl with long blond hair and blue eyes, she was married to my grandfather Nicholas who was 15 years older than her; by her parents who were business people in a small town. They had eight children and one girl that died in early childhood. Some stories say that she tried to run away on her wedding night but I am not sure if this is right or it is just fantasy.

They were living in a spacious house above the family store in an elegant district in the center of the city but communism came and they had their store, their house and their lands confiscated; leaving them afraid, confused, ashamed, humiliated, and with nothing to live on.

My grandfather started work as a waiter and my father who was the first-born boy started working early when he was only 14 years old in order to help support the family. Elisabeth had no other skills than being a wife and a mother.

She was a cold mother and a cold grandmother who showed no affection, calling us only to ask for money. I do not recall ever receiving even a small gift or a hug from her, compared to my grandfather who was extremely warm, kind and affectionate with everyone.

They never recovered from the disruptive trauma created by communism in their lives. My grandfather died of diabetes in just 4 years after his loss. His wife Elisabeth became a hoarder of newspapers and other useless objects in a desperate need for safety and comfort. She died 3 years after her husband also of diabetes. I believe that her life being so drastically changed that, it was all too much for her to handle. It may also be that at the time of her arranged marriage she was in love with another man and married my grandfather only to obey her parents never to find true happiness in her life.

It is through stories like these and through personal deeds that we shape our legacy in the world, and the thought that we may completely misinterpret the lives of those that are most close to our heart truly saddens me. As a woman of faith and love, I feel deeply connected to the women in my family walking before me on the path of life and I feel it is my duty to be compassionate, grateful, and honoring to all of them.

The legacy message I share from my heart to my Grandmothers is:

"Grandmothers of my heart, your love, your sorrow, your smiles and your memories all live ingrained in me. I love you and I say my goodbyes to you until we meet again. May you find your peace wherever you may be. God, bless you!

The message that I share from my heart to yours is:

"You are who you are today because of your roots. Make peace with your ancestors. Honor them. Receive their blessings."

About the Author

Danielle Nistor is a Messenger and a Divine Connector for the Divine Feminine, gift that was entrusted to her in the year 2000. During a spiritual pilgrimage the Divine Mother appeared to Danielle and said to her in that vision: "I want you to be my messenger and bring my divine love and guidance to people."

Since then, in spite of holding a BA in International Law she decided to dedicate her whole life to spread the messages of healing and divine love. Danielle is an international, inspirational speaker and she leads groups of people to sacred places for healing, transformation and spiritual evolution. She is also a best seller writer and the creator of the CD series 'Connecting with the Divine.'

Danielle created HealingInSpirit™ a personalized spiritual healing technique that weaves channeling, clearing, healing and blessing to bring rapid breakthroughs and miracles in people's lives. She has been featured on many radio and television channels internationally.

Her belief is that The Universe loves us exactly as we are; valued and unique, divine beings of love, and light.

A long-time journeyer to sacred places, she invites her life's experiences to continuously re-define and transform her to be able to better serve the people, and the Divine. Danielle's life mission is to impact at least 1 billion people on earth by connecting them with divine love, their own true essence and their life purpose.

She is committed to truth, self-expression and respect. She is committed to empower you to shine in your Authentic Self in order to achieve your life purpose with ease and grace.

To learn more about Danielle and to connect with her:

650-224-9467
Danielle@DanielleNistor.com
http://DanielleNistor.com/
http://www.healingmessagesoflove.com/
https://www.facebook.com/Danielle.Nistor
https://www.facebook.com/DanielleNistorFanPage
https://www.linkedin.com/in/Danielle-Nistor
https://www.youtube.com/channel/UCw_OYcZLhbehWPWTXG1gLow

Legacies of Connection, Intention and Purpose

PROFOUND IMPRINTS
By: Susan State

Profound imprints that shape our view of life take place every day if we are willing to take the time to observe them. They are traces left often by some inconsequential daily occurrence, and, if you are lucky, by a simple event so profound that it changes the way you see things forever.

We all have influencers in our life. To a large degree, they are our family. This group provides fodder for a wide breadth of emotions, scars, care and leadership. When I count the number of reflective instances in which my life was directed in some of the most meaningful ways, it was Ganny, my grandmother, who was at that helm.

Ganny had lived through the Great Depression. No doubt, that time triggered countless nights of anxiety as my grandparents wondered how to put food on the table and a roof over their heads. Like so many, she had lost her home because of it, so she took on a tedious job the Depression after to recoup some of the loss endured. Even though that period would challenge her to the core, she would eventually see that the bank home loan was paid in full, even though they gave back their home. **That terrible Depression never changed her outlook. She chose to always see the best in people, to be joyous in her life better than anyone I knew, and to love her grandchildren with every breath of her being.**

Ganny was always aware of everything and everyone around her, which is something I was learning by seven, was an essential tool in life. She could walk into a room of strangers and walk away with intimate details of their lives tucked away in her memory; because she was so approachable, should would often dispense advice, not because she was bossy, but because people were drawn to her intense desire to do the right thing. People saw that in her words of advice helped situations or relationships become better simply because she took the time to listen and respond to them.

I admired most in her desire to be part of her entire world, not just the one she lived in. It was because she was considerate and opens to everyone around her that drew people to her. It was that mannerism that opened her up to experiences so many would have simply missed. Those traits, it turned out, would play into one day of my life in a very profound way.

It was fall in Oakland, California and I was seven years old. Ganny lived near Lake Merritt in Oakland next to a vacant hill that provided hours of entertainment to my sister, my brother and me. She would find a large box, cut it into flat pieces, and we would slide down to the bottom of that hill in sheer delight. Then, we would run back up the hill and do it again, and again, until we were all utterly exhausted, but on this day, there were no flat pieces of cardboard because she was busy getting the three of us ready to go to Fairyland.

Fairyland was next to the Duck Park on Lake Merritt, and once through the entrance, we were always greeted by Puff the Magic

Dragon, who signaled the beginning of our adventure through the storybook theme park. We each had our own plastic yellow key that would turn to the right in the storybook box in front of the exhibit, and a story or song to describe what we were looking at. All three of us would remember the countless trips to Fairyland with Ganny as some of the most fun moments of our lives; so on this day, the excitement of the trip was, per usual, high. It never got old going to Fairyland with Ganny.

Ganny had never learned to drive. It didn't really made sense that someone with such quiet confidence never learned to drive, but that was part of the dichotomy of her personality. So, we always took the bus.

We watched eagerly as she got ready for the outing. She would put on a simple print dress, always with a narrow belt and a girdle underneath, nylons, gloves and a hat. She had a special drawer for her beautiful handkerchiefs, a thin drawer at the top of the dresser that was filled to the brim with dozens of handkerchiefs. She would stand there at the drawer, and carefully select one depending upon what she was wearing that day. Once placed in her pocketbook, she led us down the hill to the bus stop where we would wait with anxious anticipation for its arrival. Once seated, we would laugh and giggle about the experience that lay ahead of us.

There were two entrances on the bus; one in the front and the other in the back. We scrambled on the bus, took our seats, and we were on our way to Fairyland. As we approached the next bus stop, I looked out the window and there was an older black woman standing by herself under the bus stop sign. As the door opened, I watched as she entered the bus in the back, which was something that in-and-of-itself would have been lost on me, as it is the same entrance that we too had entered. On any other day and without the ensuing discussion that followed this day, I would never have been aware that it was a habit she was burdened with because not too many years before that it was the only entrance she could use. The fact that we too had entered the bus in the back was a decision we simply made based on convenience.

The woman at the stop was very thin, with a simple brown straight coat and a clutch handbag. It was hard to tell how old she was, and she looked much older than I suspect she really was. I remember seeing her frail figure as she started to climb the first of three steps before getting to the level where the seats were. She was slow to get onto the bus, taking careful measured steps as she entered.

It was at that moment that I glanced at the bus driver. I only saw the back of his head, so to see better, I took my eyes up to the rear-view-mirror to see his face, and I saw a look I had never seen before. His eyes were glaring back at the black woman trying to get onto the bus. She had only made it up the first two steps when his faced turned diabolical and deliberate. It was then that he calculatingly shut the door behind her and stepped on the accelerator of the bus so fast that it caused her to fall. The look on his face as he had accomplished his intended goal was chilling to me.

In a split second, Ganny was up from her seat and racing up to the bus driver. When she got up to him, she was in his face and wagging her finger and although not being able to hear what she was saying, it was obvious she was giving him a tongue-lashing. Within seconds, the bus was stopped against a curb.

Ganny rushed back to the woman who was on the floor of the bus is some shock, and her arm was bleeding. She gently helped the woman get back onto her feet and reached in her pocketbook to retrieve her freshly laundered hankie and placed it on the wound. She gathered all three of her grandchildren up, and we walked to a nearby bicycle shop that was in the distance. During that walk, my grandmother's arm was placed tenderly around the woman's shoulder, and she guided the woman to a small chair inside the shop. With the help of the bike shop owner, the wound was tended to, she was given water and we waited with her until Ganny was certain she was well enough to leave. The woman thanked Ganny for her kindness and we walked up to the next bus stop, and got on another bus to continue our trip to Fairyland.

It was a seminal moment for me. There were so many deeply embedded traits and decisions being taught to me that day. It was a beautifully touching observation of two women who were strangers juxtaposed against a racist bus driver.

We talked about it for several days as I struggled to understand why the bus driver showed so much malice; but I never had to ask why Ganny had shown so much compassion because that was something we saw every day of her life. Most seven-year-olds would have missed an opportunity to understand how complex this situation was, but because Ganny's life was spent collecting details, not just looking at the big picture, I saw it all. I saw the malice and intent of the driver, the conviction to make right what was wrong, and the compassion between two women who had never met and would never see each other again.

What Ganny had demonstrated through her actions that day was just the way she lived her life, but it changed forever mine. It was because of her that I had learned to see the details. It was because of her that I became brave. **It was because of Ganny that the woman felt love that day. And that was the greatest lesson of them all.**

What I learned from the legacy my grandmother imparted is that the most profound imprints aren't always loud or boisterous. They can be, but the most effective imprints are those that are observed during a simple gesture, a seemingly inconsequential comment, or a quiet but determined act of bravery. Some find that hard to understand. They want things to hit them over the head before they see them. Therefore, they let profound imprints slip through their hands and those simple, quiet teaching moments slide into oblivion and are lost forever.

I realized by watching the way she lived is that it isn't about "finding one's purpose" or the 'meaning of **your life**.' One of the most important life skills I have learned by this unassuming grandmother is that the greatest impact one can have in life is to live it as though every person and everything you encounter every day deserves to be seen, acknowledged, and sometimes those observations require you to act. That requires you to be brave.

Routine bravery requires you to act when it isn't necessarily comfortable to do so. Even something simple like starting a conversation with a stranger requires a certain degree of vulnerability and courage; but the outcome can yield enormous benefits. That exchanges might manifest in giving advice or taking advice, and you need to be open to whatever direction it takes you.

What is clear during all those interactions is that the accumulation of those quiet imprints can reverberate throughout all eternity. Her actions changed my life, and I hope to have lived my life in a way that my children have observed that same decorum and eventually pass that along to their children. You may not think that a **single act can be far-reaching**, but it can be. It has been decades since that day on the bus, but Ganny's actions are as important to me today as they were that day on the bus with her determined, quiet and decisive action. Profound imprints are created when you are willing to observe, strong enough to be brave and above-all, act from a place of love. Ganny, I learned that from you.

About the Author

Susan State is the founder of S L State & Associates, LLC, serving the California Building Industry as a lead consulting firm for over three decades. Susan gained a multi-dimensional approach to this industry by working with some of the larger homebuilders since the early 1970's. Some of the companies she worked for included Broadmoor Homes, Daon Corporation, and The Imperial Group. Ms. State held positions including Asst. Director of Operations, Project Manager and Vice President of Sales and Marketing. Through this hand-on experience early in her professional career, she could formulate strategies and practical experience in the home-building business, and that, combined with her strong analytic ability helped to create this firm's systematic and creative approach to market research. It is through that discipline that she learned that most matters are about art and science, which served as a mantra in her business.

S. L. State & Associates was the publisher of The State Report, a quarterly audit of construction activity occurring throughout the 9-County Bay Area and the Central Valley until sold in 2006, and is currently working on another publication to the Building Industry.

Susan is invited to speak to groups often, including PCBC, lenders, builders, developers; investors, both local and abroad. She has served as a board member of CASA in the San Ramon Valley, teaches art to neighborhood children, received honors in High School and College, was the recipient of the Daughters' of the American Revolution Award.

She is a prolific abstract artist and has sold her art at the Blackhawk Gallery in Danville. She believes that art is about capturing hidden pieces of energy that are individually perceptible, distinct and free, yet they can come together in a way that pulls them together as one. This is true of her paintings and writings. Susan's paintings are a juxtaposition of the absurdity and absolute, unpredictability and certainty, and the positives and negatives that exists in every environment.

Her original abstract paintings and writings reflect her ability to see the world . . . from her soul.

Contact Info:

Susan L State
S L State & Associates
1972 Chambers Circle
Brentwood, CA 94513
www.slstate.com
(925) 735-1000 (Office)

(925) 785-6096 (Mobile)

https://www.linkedin.com/in/susanstate/

MOTHERED FROM A DISTANCE
By: Trisha Garrett

I want to acknowledge and encourage the thousands, millions of grandmothers that stepped in to love on their grandbabies with a mother's heart in the absence of a parent. Our parent is not forgotten, however, your unselfish act to intentionally love, nurture, discipline and influence the lives of your grandbabies has changed the course of our lives for the better. You have given us a beautiful gift...you. I am speaking from first-hand experience and on behalf of all the beneficiaries we receive your gift in the spirit of love and appreciation. This is something that my grandmother did and I am so grateful. Her loving accepting presence was needed in the lives of her grandbabies. She brought a loving sweetness that was gentle and warm. Family dynamics were a little tough at times but her commitment to her grandbabies was unwavering. My grandmother would share her sweet warmth and love in a way like no other. She taught me things in a way that has had a lasting effect.

When I was two years old my mother passed away and without any thought, my grandparents stepped in. The death of my mother during child birth brought a lot of discord in the family and there were many times my brother and I would go months without seeing her. We could only experience her love from a distance. However, no matter what, my grandmother was determined to be in the life of her grandbabies. I was too young to understand the sacrifice, commitment and love that were displayed. It would be years later during times of reflection and conversations with my grandmother that I would come to know experience and see some of the puzzle pieces come together.

From a distance, my grandmother's life would have a profound impact on my life filled with lessons of unconditional love, patience, compassion and commitment. My learning's from my grandmother came from who she was being, what she stood for and her unwavering belief in God. It was the example that she lived before me as a woman, as African American woman, a black woman, a colored woman, a nigro woman born in 1918; a woman that had to leave school after the 6th grade to care for her six younger siblings and work in the cotton fields. A woman that went from witnessing and experiencing the aftermath of slavery, where her ancestors were considered three fifths of a person to experiencing a colored man for President of the United States.

The oldest of seven children, she was a woman that would out live the siblings that she helped to raise. I remember asking my grandmother what it was like to lose those closest to her. No one to reminisce with about the "good old days;" She paused, looked into the distance, her body became still and in a soft voice said, "It can feel lonely…baby you never stop missing them." I was silenced as my heart filling up with compassion. In that second I saw a woman of strength and resilience.

My grandmother knew who she was as a woman. When she walked, she held her head up high with a dignity that was infectious. One day my grandmother and I were having a conversation about marriage. I was explaining to her the importance of being in love when you get married. She listened with a smile. I interpreted the smile as yes, I agree. Now my grandmother starts in…you know being in love is good but it's not everything. You need more than just love to make a marriage last. I was shocked and in total disagreement. Clearly, she had missed it on this one. She went on to explain that she agreed to marry my grandfather not because she was initially in love but based on mutual respect and their binding commitment to each other that would last over 55 years, until the death of my grandfather.

My grandmother was a proud woman and I come from a long line of women that took pride in loving their babies with a strong commitment to family. I was blessed to have not only my grandmother apart of my life but my great grandmother, Suzamamma. My great, great grandmother, Big Mamma, was in my life just for a brief period of time while my grandmother cared for her and me before her passing. I remember when my great, great grandmother came to live with my grandmother.

I often wonder what her life was like as she wore the clothing of a slave. She always wore a scarf on her head, long skirt with an apron and blouse. She had cataracts and was legally blind. I remember my grandmother getting me dressed one morning and telling Big Mamma how pretty I looked. Big Mamma curious, called me into the living room because she wanted to see. As I walked in she was sitting in the chair and she called me closer. As I approached her she kept saying I was beautiful. Baby turn around so I can see you real good. I asked my grandmother how she know what I look like if she can't see me. Big Mamma chimed in and said, "Oh baby, I can see you." I could feel the radiance of her loving words piercing through my body, instilling a confidence and a sense of pride, I felt beautiful. In that moment, nothing else mattered, Big Mamma gave me the amazing gift of being seen and being heard.

I remember my grandmother taking care of me around the age of three years old. I felt content, safe and loved. My grandmother had a daily routine of getting up fixing breakfast and immediately cleaning the kitchen. Part of her cleanup routine she would sweep the floor. This was especially exciting for me because I had a special job of holding the dust pan as she would sweep the loose trash into it. Wow! I felt so accomplished. I had become a master at holding the dust pan at just the right angle so that with a couple of strokes of the broom everything was in the dust pan.

You must understand, I had big dreams of not just holding the dust pan but was ready to be promoted to the next level. I would watch, study my grandmother as she would bend over, pick up the dust pan, stand up and very steadily with one hand walk the dust pan of trash over to the larger trash container and dump it. Every day I would get so inspired watching her. I knew I could do it. So, I began asking her to let me do, I can do it, then I would add a "please" on there to show her that I could even ask 'like a big girl.'

Finally, the time is now…my grandmother agreed to let me walk the dust pan with the loose trash to the larger trash container. I was nervous and excited!! I had studied my grandmother and I was ready. She swept the loose trash into the dust pan and I squatted to picked it up with one hand, my grandmother rushed to say, baby, use both hands? Confused as to why she was telling me that? I had study her and she only used one hand. It was all happening so fast. I proceed to pick up the dust pan with one hand and just a couple is steps away from the larger trash container, and stand up. My heart is beating fast with anticipation…and I did it…oops; I almost did it…as my grandmother is saying, "baby two hands."

Something happened and before I knew it the loose trash was back on the floor along with the dust pan. Just as quickly as the loose trash hit the floor my grandmother is telling me let's do it again and use two hands. She continues to mumble in a sweet soft tone…" **when you get old enough to really do something you are not going to be anywhere in site…. come on, go ahead and pick it up"** I didn't understand what she was talking about because all I cared about was getting the trash into the big trash container. I did it the way my grandmother had encouraged me to do and I did it! From there I was on the fast track and began to take over sweeping one small section of the kitchen floor while my grandmother would clean the entire kitchen.

Solid in whom she was being, over time my grandmother would teach a powerful lesson. That by slowing down it would allow me to easily connect and listen to my heart/intuition for direction. Using both hands would bring balance and the open heart to hear a different perspective even when I feel that I am 'right.' Connecting, listening, hearing and staying open disbands resistance in the atmosphere; opening the door to invite in new possibilities.

As an adult in my late 20's, my grandparents moved back to Texas and I would visit them at least once a year. It was always a joy to visit. We would spend time with extended family. My grandmother always cooked my favorite foods. To sit and talk for hours was our favorite thing to do together. She would tell me story after story about her life and different family members. I would learn so much about her as a woman, a wife, a mother. I would share with her the details of my relationships. Although she did not tell me what to do, she was clear about what she would allow or not allow in her relationship with my grandfather; **Quick to share the importance of compromise, which would be followed up with a lesson in self-respect and boundaries.**

During my visits, we would always have a special time together after the soap operas were off for the day. I would sit and watch them with her as she would attempt to catch me up on the lives of each character. I recall a time when we were watching the soaps and my grandmother gets up and goes into the kitchen and comes back with a bag of green bean that she begins to snap. I offer to help and my grandmother says, "No that's ok baby you just sit there and relax." I insisted, as I get up and go get a bowl from the kitchen to help. Before I knew it, we had finished snapping the green beans and her large bowl was full. My grandmother reaches for my bowl and as I hand it to her I begin to laugh, she looked in my half full bowl and looks back at me, she chuckles and says, "Girl you ain't worth a dime." Humorous Reflection; prophecy fulfilled I guess, I lost my domestic enthusiasm somewhere along the way.

One of my grandparent's favorite things to do together was fishing. They would go out on the water and fish for hours. Come home clean the fish and fry it up. I was always intrigued by my grandfather. He did not have a formal education but I thought he was one of the smartest men around. I was fascinated how he was so in synch with nature. His ability to read the behavior of animals to accurately predict the next move of nature was impressive. I was mesmerized watching him play dominos. I never saw anyone count their dominos faster than my grandfather. He refused to play with me since I could never count my dominos fast enough. He would get frustrated. I quickly learned to stop him from fussing at me, all I had to do was say, Papa I love you. Each time, I could hear his hear melt and he would say "Baby I love you too." Frustration would dissipate.

Years later my grandfather was diagnosed with lung cancer. I get "that" the call that my grandfather is probably not going to make it. I jump on a plane and fly to Texas. When I arrive at the hospital and enter my grandfather's room, my grandmother is standing over my grandfather with a cold cloth to his forehead trying to keep him comfortable. My grandfather is going in and out of consciousness struggling for every breath with long pauses between each breath. My grandfather looks up and sees me, he says to me, "Hi baby, how you doing?" Baby you looks good, you looks good baby. Then immediately back to struggling to breath. It's been a few hours and my grandfather is not getting better.

I ask my grandmother how long, did she want to stay, because it was getting late and we should probably leave and grab dinner on the way home. **My grandmother looked up at me and softly said, "Baby I'm not leaving."** I explained to her that she also needed her rest. As she stood over my grandfather continuing to attend to his needs she gently said to me lovingly, baby, this is what you do…this is what you do; her eyes softly glancing at me as she turned back to attending to my grandfather. It was not just the words my grandmother spoke; it was something in the tone of her voice, gentle, loving but firm. My heart sank because I realized there was something happening and I wasn't quite getting it.

Clearly, that was the wrong thing to ask. I sat quietly wondering what to do next. I began to reflect on stories my grandmother shared with me over the years about their relationship. I think this is where you need more than being in love, comes into play. They were sharing something between the two of them that I could not fully comprehend. It was beautiful, sweet and heartbreaking all mixed together. I see two people that are more than in love. It was trust, honoring commitment even when it did feel good, respect and a slow tearing apart of their souls after bonding together for 55 years.

I was witnessing what it is to love, respect and stand in your commitment with every part of your being from the inside out. That moment has stayed with me. I tuck it away deep in my heart knowing that new wisdoms will continue to unfold. She was committed to my grandfather just as much as he was committed to her. Once she shared with me that even though they had been married a long time just when she thought she knew my grandfather like the back of her hand, he would behave in a way that would surprise her. She went on to tell me that she trusted my grandfather with her life. There were times when she had been sick and she didn't worry because she knew that no matter what, my grandfather was there for her. **Commitment and respect was still the foundation of their relationship which was woven together in love.**

My grandmother out lived all of her siblings and the only one to remain married to the same man. She had such a powerful impact in our family that my cousins would call her frequently to check up on her and give her the latest happenings in their lives. Some of the best times were when a bunch of us cousins would travel to Texas to visit her. As a small child, it was the relationship with my grandmother that kept me connected to my aunties, great aunties, great uncles and tons of cousins on my mother's side of the family. **It would be the bond of those relationships established in early childhood that would sustain my family relationships because of her determination to be in our life.**

In the recent years, the awareness of the amazing impact she had on my life as a woman. I would always tell my grandmother that I loved her and the words seem so limiting. Early in my life she wanted to make sure that I knew she loved me. Later in my life I wanted to make sure she knew just how much I loved her. I called my grandmother in January 2017 excited to let her know that I had finalized my schedule and I was coming to see her soon. With the loss of hearing and dementia accelerating, the past year was difficult to have a phone conversation. However, today I'm especially blessed, she knew who was and my heart was full of joy. In her usual style, she did what she had done from the time that I can remember she started telling me all the things she was grateful for, in spite of the dementia.

Being in chronic pain did not stop her from sharing all that she was grateful for daily. I was eager to share with her that I would see her in two months. She was always quick to tell me, baby now you know you don't have to call, just come. You can come at any time. This is home. I thanked her and repeated that I would visit in two months. There was a silence on the other end of the phone. Very concerned, my grandmother said, "Well baby, I'm not sure I going to remember that far away." Full of compassion, my heart smiled as I told her Momo don't worry, I can remind you; I can keep reminding you if you forget." There was a joy and uplifting of her spirit as she said, "Okay baby, yes, okay baby that would be good." We shared a sweet connection. My heart was happy. This would be our last conversation. After suffering a stroke, two weeks earlier, on February 1, 2017, my grandmother would transition at the age of 98.

Mrs. L. V. Scott, my grandmother, better known as "Momo" is a woman that I'm grateful to have had in my life. She loved her grandbabies, her family and made sure that we all knew she loved us whether it was up close or from a distance.

Encouragement to Grandmothers

As tribute to my grandmother, who would have been 99 years old today, August 28, 2017. I want to encourage all the loving grandparents that are struggling to have relationships with their grandbabies. Hold fast to your commitment. Allow your bounce-back muscle to mature. Trust your instincts. I want to encourage you to not give up. They need you and you need them. Keep expressing your love for your grandbabies even if you have to do it from a distance. Their hearts WILL hear you!

About the Author

Trisha is the Owner and Executive Producer of BriteLiteTV Channel which is on the recently launched RHGTV Network. BriteLite TV Programming reinforces that You Matter, You are

Enough and You are Powerful through; Inspiration, Education and Personal Empowerment. Trisha is the Host of the "Trisha Garrett Show". Articulating her creative flair "Trimiah Presents…" was created to bring diverse expressions of entertainment; both shows are syndicated on VoiceAmericaTV.com.

Trisha is an International Amazon Best-Selling Co-Author *(Come Out of Hiding and Shine)*. Trisha's a frequent guest on Talk Radio shows and Panelist for Speaker Talent Search where opportunities for the candidates to be seen, heard and expand their audience.

Core to her passion, for the 20 years of Trisha working for Fortune 100 Companies in Silicon Valley several of those years she managed Girl's Technology Day at Intel Corporation. The event introduced, simulated, and encouraged over 100 girls each year from underserved communities' interest in (STEM) careers.

A drive and on purpose to help women stand up, live bigger, and thrive deepened as she volunteered with a non-profit organization, which helped women to assimilate into mainstream society. Trisha headed up the mentoring and coaching program while providing educational, career and life coaching for single mothers.

As a certified life coach Trisha is providing programs that empowers women to design the life they truly desire to live stand in their greatness and to bring positive change to communities around the globe.

trisha@britelitetv.com
www.facebook.com/britelitetv
www.twitter.com/britelitetv
www.instagram.com/britelitetv

MY FAVORITE HEALER
GRANDMA TINA
By: Lorraine Giordano

Growing up I was fortunate to enjoy both of my grandmas until their passing in their early 90's. My Grandma Millie and Grandma Tina both served as a port of refuge and calm when waters got rough with my parents growing up. Both of my grandmas excelled in their ability to not only share robust flavors in the dishes they cooked with warm smiles, but also had a special knack in adding spices and unique personal ingredients to the stories from their past difficulties and successes. I'm deeply grateful for learning the art and importance of sharing stories about family and love from them. I'm honored to share the story about my Grandma Tina with you.

My Abuela—Grandma Tina—passed away on May 19, 2015, in Frisco, Texas. She was 92. Beautiful, strong, determined, highly intuitive, and complex, she lived a rich life. Rich—not in money, but love. As I sat at her service and listened to my mom, aunts, and cousins share insights and memories about her, it dawned on me that my Grandma Tina had been a formidable energy healer.

Grandma Tina and I never talked about energy work or my alternative healing practice – Inspired To Health. She knew I'd left the financial industry after over twenty years to start my own business helping women feel less stress, focus on their health, but I never went into detail. I didn't think she would understand and might be concerned about leaving the stability of corporate America. I also didn't get into specifics that I work with my clients and enjoy writing about connecting to down there – the sacral chakra that relates to emotions, creativity and passion. My grandma was a bit old school so 'down there' was primarily about sex and having babies. We talked more about food. She excitedly shared recipes like lentil soup and roasted chicken and tips about the tasty herbs and spices she cooked with.

We also talked about her life. My favorite moments with her were when we hung out, one-on-one, and she told me intimate stories about how she'd met my grandfather or tough times when she was a little girl. She often pulled out her collection of jewelry, sharing the history of a pretty ring or necklace she'd received fifty years ago or a trinket she'd bought on her own or been given as a birthday or Christmas gift. After our chats, she always sat me down to a home-cooked dinner. Her food was incredible. She made the best *arroz con pollo* with fried plantains I've ever tasted.

It was only after my Abuela's passing that, I realized she shared universal truths about life that echoed many of the best energy healers I read or heard about. Here are three examples:

1. **Manifest your desires**

Orphaned at two, with no formal education, my grandma possessed an incredible ability to manifest her wishes, including supporting her five children as a single mother, saving enough money for a piece of jewelry that caught her attention, and taking exotic trips to Hawaii, Italy, and the Caribbean. She often advised me to close my eyes and focus on what I wanted with all my heart. It didn't matter if it didn't show up right away. She stressed how important it was for me to believe that whatever I wanted was on its way and to keep seeing and feeling it. Did her approach at times cause some ruffled feathers in my family? Sure, but she manifested her desires and made things happen.

"By focusing on what you don't have, that situation of not-having will also be your reality. You attract to yourself things or people that are the equivalent of your current state of being, or 'vibration.'"—Esther and Jerry Hicks

2. **Connect to your Feminine Energy**

My Grandma Tina was a gorgeous lady on the inside and out. Even when she reached 90 years of age she looked like she was 70. The most glamorous at family events, she lit up a room with her luminous glow and bright smile, always framed with robust lipstick. She knew how to take care of and adore her feminine side because it made her feel good. Besides accessorizing with brilliant jewels, she kept her skin soft with special creams, spritzed her wrists and throat with luscious scents, and took excellent care of her hair and nails, even during her last days. She often stressed that women needed to remember they were women, not men. Although I don't think I ever heard my Abuela use the word "goddess", her actions indicated she knew the importance of treating herself like one.

"The Sacred Bombshell knows that her creative energy is a catalyst. She remembers her womb wisdom."—Abiola Abrams

3. Do it with Love

At my grandma's service, my mom shared that my Abuela often cooked tamales—always using quality ingredients—and sold them to support her family. Even though people said her tamales were more expensive than others, many of those people continued to order from her because her tamales tasted extra delicious. Blessed with the ability to cook and bake, she shared her gift with others to bring abundance to her family. For as long as I can remember, Tina was a phenomenal cook, eliciting exclamations of glee and demands for more from family and friends. Her most demanded food was *carinamanolas*, or "footballs", a Panamanian comfort food. She also baked delicious cakes, especially her sweet yellow cake recipe known as "grandma special". I believe her food tasted so good because she infused her dishes with love.

"Doing what you love is the cornerstone of having abundance in your life."—Dr. Wayne Dyer

I miss my grandma. I'm filled with eternal thanks for my time with her and all the memories. Even in her 90's her spirit was energetic and youthful. It makes me smile to think she's reunited and cooking up a storm for my grandpa, Popi; Tia Carmen; and Tio Jorge. She won't be listed in any books with the energy shifters of our time, but her energy dramatically transformed those close to her.

From her example, I've come to believe, whether we realize it or not, we're all energy healers in our own unique way.

Remember to add these potent ingredients of wisdom from My Grandmother, the energy healer, to **your daily life** to Manifest Your Dreams:

1. Visualize in vivid detail your desires and use your imagination
2. Connect to your Feminine Energy
3. Do it with Love

About the Author

Lorraine Giordano is an intuitive energy healer shifting the way women connect to down there. Lorraine is passionate about sharing ways for women to connect to their own healing and creative energy, and highlighting opportunities to bridge the gap from dis-ease to finding their personal healthy way in their daily life. She previously worked in the financial industry developing financial software products and experienced many health challenges over two decades.

Due to the threat of losing her uterus in 2008, she realized how much she didn't know about her body – especially her female reproductive organs. Not willing to give up her uterus, she put Operation Save Uterus into action and learned how to reclaim her health. As a holistic energy healer, with her uterus intact, she now helps women connect to their own healing ability and understand the importance and power of down there.

Lorraine is an Usui Reiki Master and certified in Quantum Energy Transformation, Quantum Touch and Integrated Energy Therapy. Lorraine won the Best of Award 2015 by Thumbtack for Reiki Masters in NYC and in 2013 & 2016 she won a bronze Stevie

Award - Women Helping Women. Her newsletter has won the Constant Contact All-Star Award the past three years. She's contributed to the Huffington Post and is currently writing her memoir on her healing journey. She is the host on The Womb Happy Hour radio show on Voice America Health & Wellness.

info@inspiredtohealth.net

The Infamous One: On Beyond the Magic Grandma
By: Nina Price

When I think of my grandmother, I always smile. She was my first best friend. From the time, I was born; I knew that she knew exactly who I was. She totally 'got' me. I was the next version of her, and she knew it. I was her only granddaughter and I was her favorite. She sewed me dresses, and taught me to play fifteen types of Solitaire. She practiced the piano with me, and taught me to be a good sport. Even as an old lady, she was full of mischief. She had a big twinkle in her eye and a biting sense of humor.

Even though she was less than five-foot-tall - in heels, and I've always been quite tall – she told everyone that when she was young, she was tall and blonde like I was. I believed her. My cousins, who were ten and fifteen years older than I, weren't fooled for a minute. In fact, they persuaded me that there was no way she could have *ever* looked like me; but **I didn't care that she never looked like me, I was her favorite – and she was my advocate. She believed in me.**

My grandmother had a tea party at her house every Thursday afternoon for my brother and me. She lived a block away from our school and we used to run over to her house after school on Thursdays. Her tea parties were really cute. She always served tea and Linzer cookies. We were each allowed to bring a friend. She loved her children and her grandchildren, and she savored the time she got to spend with us.

My grandmother knew what I was thinking even when I did not. I remember her telling me when I phoned her from college several states away, that she didn't like the look on my face. I'm convinced that she was responsible for nurturing the confidence I've always felt. She believed that I was smart and capable of succeeding at anything I put my mind to, and so I was. Her confidence in me plus my own drive, allowed me to be a straight A student. **She expected me to be outstanding, so I was.**

Today I'm a grandmother of two teen aged girls. I became a grandmother at age 42; not exactly what I had in mind for myself, or for my daughter, who had just finished her first year in college. At the time, I wrote a short story which shared my feelings about becoming a grandmother, called "The Concept Sucks."

Here's an excerpt:

"Becoming a grandmother just happens to you, there's nothing you do to make it happen. No planning. No strategizing. No elaborate tactics. You could even say it's done to you. You do nothing, and as a consequence of others' choices and behaviors, your identity changes and like it or not, you change as a result."

Babies are born every day to women of all ages; young girls, teenagers, young women in their 20's and 30's, even middle aged women in their 40's and 50's; before the door of their fertility shuts in their faces. And their mothers all get to become grandmothers; the mothers who've waited for years for the privilege, the ones who've almost given up hope, the ones who just couldn't wait and even mothers like me, who didn't even know what hit them; who felt they were too young, and weren't even considering it. After all, some women our age were just having their first children! I felt as though I had utterly failed as a mother, becoming a grandmother at 42. I'm not sure why I felt responsible for my daughter's choices. I had taught her everything I was supposed to – but it felt as though I hadn't. **On a September afternoon at one o'clock I arrived at a small hospital in another state and met my granddaughter, one hour after she was born, and completely fell in love with her.**

I spent the next week bonding with my granddaughter. I hugged her, cuddled her, rocked her, gave her kisses, sang to her, changed her diapers, and told her to grow up so that we could get into mischief. She didn't know that she had done this to me – made me a grandmother; changed my identity. We became fast friends and I did the same thing when her sister arrived twenty months later.

Everyone in the entire family encouraged my daughter to stay in college, and she did – graduating with honors in Biochemistry, and then graduating from Veterinary school, with two school aged kids, a husband and a couple of puppies.

Until they became teenagers my granddaughters used to get very excited when they knew I was coming to visit. I would be walking in the airport looking for them and they would run up, and hurl themselves into my arms full of big hugs. One granddaughter proclaimed, **"My grandma is better than Santa Claus**! Santa only comes *once* a year and brings presents!" The other granddaughter's favorite part of my visits was that I took them on shopping 'sprees.' I enjoyed being a magic grandma and worked hard to make sure that I was maintaining my magic perception, I wasn't willing to let the "opinion polls" change. **I liked being thought of as "better than Santa Claus." I started calling myself "the infamous Grandma Nina" and was told that I used big words. Now that they're teenagers they just call me "the Infamous One." which I rather like.**

When she was about twelve, my younger granddaughter drew a comic strip called *"**The Non-Stuffy Grandmother**"* in which she positioned me against the "stuffy grandmothers" who were all drawn with little buns on their heads, sitting in rocking chairs with knitting needles – an expression of true, heartfelt love. I felt honored and loved.

"My grandma is bringing presents – because that's her job!" the older granddaughter told her friend; but in truth I did more than just spoil them. We travelled, we played, we ice skated, we snow-shoed and we went to the beach, rode scary roller coasters, took road trips. We did things kids love to do, we had family reunions, we had "Cousins Camp." and we had lots of family fun whenever we got together. When the granddaughters came to our house they always spent as much time as possible in our pool. They would have slept in the pool if we'd let them. **One time they gave me a refrigerator magnet that says "what happens at Grandma's stays at Grandma's"** – I felt honored. My goal was to create cherished memories of the fun we had together.

Even though my grandmother was always there for me, she never specifically said so to me. She just modeled how to be a grandmother and without realizing it. I copied some of the magic I had felt from that relationship with my own granddaughters. My granddaughters grew up in a very different time than I did. I wanted to be sure that my granddaughters knew that I was there for them no matter what, and that I would always love them. I told them as much, very directly. I also told them that what I wished for more than anything was that they would smile whenever they thought of me; just like I do when I think of my grandmother.

I also remembered from my own growing up years that when I became a teenager the magic of my relationship with my grandmother was not as important to me as it had been when I was younger, and likewise my teenaged granddaughters became less interested in spending time with me as they got older. Even though I understood this, it still hurt. Their friends, boyfriends, the prom and all the other things teenage girls care about became more important to them. Gone were the days of excitement when grandma shows up. Gone was the desire to visit Grandma's house, gone was the fun, frolic and mischief that we had together when they were younger. It was a new kind of empty nest; granddaughters become teenagers and don't care about you anymore. Rather than long phone conversations, our communications became terse Facebook messages. Rather than shopping "sprees" with Grandma, they just want gift cards so they can shop with their friends. Grandma is no longer "magic," and she has to work *really* hard to stay relevant in the opinion polls, if she matters at all.

I didn't really know who I was transitioning into. I knew I wasn't the "Magic Grandma" anymore – but who am I now? I felt like "Unrequited Love Grandma." Who do I want to become?

I want to be "The Infamous One"– the 21st century version of my grandmother. The Grandma who makes you giggle when you see her face on Facebook, or hear her on the phone, because she's so unstuffy she verges on outrageous. She's cool. She's stylish. She listens to cool music, watches cool films, plays cool games, and takes you to cool places. When she's around we're always all having fun. I want them to smile when they think of me because I can be cute, mischievous, playful and even kind of a brat. **I want them to smile because: they remember that I'm their**

supporter, their cheerleader, and that I'll believe in them, even when they don't believe in themselves. I'm fiercely loyal, and I love them unconditionally, even while expecting them to be outstanding.

Tips to Creating an Infamous Legacy of your own:

How do you want your grandchildren to think of you?

What do you need to do now to create that legacy?

About the Author

Nina Price is 'The Queen of Midlife Transformation.' She is quite simply, not done yet. With an M.B.A. from the University of Michigan, she is a former Silicon Valley high tech marketing exec who after twenty years in the computer industry learned that 'it was time to do something else.' In 2001 she 'pushed her own reset button' and reinvented herself as a midlife success coach and board certified healthcare professional (a licensed acupuncturist and master herbalist;) so she could solve more kinds of problems as she serves women tackling the transformations that come with midlife and beyond. Nina lives in the Silicon Valley with her husband. She has two grown daughters, two granddaughters and four 'additional' grandchildren. For fun, she is a radio DJ who hosts a weekly music show, she is also a voice actor who produces audiobooks for Audible.

Email Address: ninapricelac@gmail.com
Phone number: 650-424-8783
Website: www.ninaprice.com
Blog: www.midlifewithoutcrisis.com
Face book Pages: Midlife Without Crisis, Turn Heads After 50
LinkedIn Page: Nina Price Twitter handle: @NinaPriceLAc
YouTube Channel: TheNinaPrice

ACTIONS SPEAK LOUDER THAN WORDS
By: Pamala Hunter Smith

Is forty-two too young to become a grandmother? I thought so. In fact, I was downright bewildered at the thought. Grandmothers were supposed to have short gray hair, drive a station wagon, wear dresses below the knee, and dating was out of the question. None of that looked like me. Throughout my daughter's pregnancy I experienced an almost unbearable inner turmoil. Anxiety from my own sense of insecurity was mixed with a curiosity about what it would be like. Being called grandmother, or worse yet granny held no warm place in my heart. Whenever the subject of grandchildren would come up in discussion, I can remember asking (often to the consternation of anyone within earshot) what was so special about them. Both of my maternal grandparents were dead before I was born.

My dad's parents lived in a small town outside of Chicago, and it was my misfortune that by the time I was born not only did they have too many grandchildren to count, but they were afraid to fly. My dad was the youngest male in a family consisting of eleven children, and everyone had kids. Our bi-annual treks to visit them felt more like paying homage to royalty. We all stood in line to get our customary words of encouragement, questions about our grades, and a comment about how much we had grown. Perhaps I was just too young to remember more of the intimate times, or perhaps, there were none. Our "visits" were over almost as soon as they started, to make sure all of us had gotten a turn. Then we were off to have some real fun – catching lightening bugs and putting them in a jar.

By the time I was nine years old, my grandparents had all passed away. When my children were five and nine, my mother suffered a massive stroke that totally changed our roles and family dynamics. For the remaining six years of her life, the woman I affectionately deemed "the whirling dervish" was no longer able to leap tall buildings in a single bound, nor was she able to mentor me on the qualities I felt I needed to have in my later years. **My perception of what a grandparent was all about was based on an incomplete model; I had no real frame of reference. I did not yet understand, or grasp, that the unsaid is often more important than what is.**

From the very first moment our eyes met, my oldest grandchild, captured my heart. The questions I harbored about what made little beings so special were answered without words. It was almost like an invisible cord tethered us together – instantly. Time stood still. The air in the delivery room seemed to have a new and sweeter aroma. My heart fluttered and there was an internal giggle that I had never experienced. The witnessing of the birth of a little one (by another) is an experience too precious to miss and almost too hard to describe. Over the next eleven years, more little people were added to my brood. **Although I never found a grandmother's manual nor had the benefit of models to emulate, loving them was as natural as breathing. I came to know that it was never about how I was supposed to act, or look, but all about how I might enrich their lives.**

By the time grandchild number five was born, a period of turmoil in my life rushed in like a flood. Within an eighteen-month window of time, the sudden death of my sister, was followed by the costly closure of my business and finally the end of a ten-year marriage. For the first time in my life, I was shaken to the core. Literally all the stuff, that I had envisioned leaving to my children and grandchildren was lost. Peeking out from the ashes, thoughts of my babies compelled me to take inventory of my life and my legacy. What I wanted to leave for them became less important than the condition I wanted to leave them in. Just entering my early fifties, the impact ultimately that I wanted to have on all their lives began to take shape and provide fuel for the next leg of my journey. It was always very important to me that I be present in their lives. But driving them to practice, and cheering on the sidelines of their sports and extracurricular activities was no longer enough. How I could equip them, arm them, and position them for a life worth living became my chief concern.

The day my oldest grandson relayed the gut wrenching details of the "conversation" the school vice principal had with him sparked something in me. Things were said to him and about him that didn't even seem proper to think. A few months earlier, my daughter had been diagnosed with lupus – the same disease that caused my sisters untimely death. If ever there was a time that emotions were raw, this was it. The comments that were said cut deep. My grandson was new to the school, and for some reason, appeared to be singled out. In the first few weeks of school, he was pegged as most likely to fail by the administration staff. Again, they didn't know or perhaps would not have cared what he was going through at home. It was hard to believe that someone entrusted with the care of children could be so callous and cavalier to "predict" that if he even made it to high school, he would most likely not graduate. I knew then that my delayed goal of returning to school had to be taken off the shelf, not only for me, but for my grandchildren as well. **I had come to know that people don't believe what you say as much as they believe what you *do*. I purposed then, not just to encourage them to go after their dreams, but to show them how to do it.** As my mother would always say, "actions speak louder than words".

My first step was to share my goal of going back to school out loud with each of them one by one. My family's initial response varied (depending on their age), but seemed to take no one by surprise. It was too soon for them to grasp the deeper meaning and my motives though. **The first major adjustment was learning how to carve out time to study. Instead of telling them I needed to hit the books, I began to invite them over to study with me.** Over the years, it became another way to create deeper bonds and mutual respect. One of my granddaughters has a gift for technology and became my tutor when I needed to know how to work a new application or computer program. As I learned how to use the latest bibliography software, I would share that information with them. When I got a handy essay outline or brainstorming template, I would find a way to weave it into a discussion. Much like I have always suggested to them, when my grades were posted from classes, they were made public in my house. It was all part of my plan. I wanted them to see what focus on a goal looked like - what it felt like. How to eat the proverbial elephant, one bite at a time. **I was trying to inspire them, they were in turn inspiring me.**

The first academic achievement (Health Coaching certificate) was met with congratulations; proud of you Googie! It was when I decided to push further and was accepted into a 4-year program that I really got their attention. **Slowly the conversations about school and higher education were not one sided, but they were asking questions, and most importantly beginning to believe**

that they could do it too. Late night texts between me and a grandchild became common as I embarked upon my studies. "Googs, what are you doing up so late"? My response was usually, "doing homework". To that I would be delighted to hear back "me too".

In September 2016, at the age of 62, I graduated with a Bachelors of Arts & Sciences from Goddard College in Vermont. Although I was initially attracted to the school culture and academic philosophy, what also interested me was the design of the learning program. It required me to be on campus for the first segment of each semester and live in a dorm. The memories and experiences that were created will last a lifetime. Each time I went, what was equally important to me was that my grandchildren would be able to see themselves in me. I would text them what I was doing, send them pictures of the cafeteria, my dorm room, and the beautiful snow-covered buildings. **It was a way for me to continue to fan the flames – to continue to give them a taste of what could be for them.** A few days after I graduated, my oldest granddaughter moved into her dorm room and shortly thereafter, began her freshman year at one of the California State universities. **Four months later, as I could hardly contain my joy, I witnessed my oldest grandson (the one who was not "supposed" to graduate from high school) graduate from college. What a blessing it has been to be present for their journeys and to see their lives unfold. My legacy to them was to let them see that actions speak louder than words.**

What one core value, precious principle, or character trait that if embraced by your loved one's would groom them for a life worth living? Further, how are you demonstrating that quality; what are you doing to model that in your own life for them? I encourage you to strive to be both transparent and relentless. Be what you are hoping they become in the face of and despite adversity.

Allow them to see you climb your mountains on purpose! My legacy to my grands has been to let them see that what we *do* speaks volumes about who we *are*. Indeed, actions speak louder than words.

About the Author

Perhaps the experience of growing up in a historic Victorian home with her artist mother and realtor father are what drew **Pamala Smith** into a career in real estate. She was surrounded by colorful tiffany lamps, cozy bay windows and oak inlaid parquet floors.

Originally licensed as a real estate salesperson in 1979, she also enjoyed much success over the years as a loan officer (residential and commercial properties) and as an area manager/ trainer for a national real estate franchise company.

Pam has been passionate about both a healthy home and a healthy body all her life. A family member's life altering experience compelled her to return to school and obtain professional training in health and wellness. She obtained a Certificate in Health Coaching from The Institute for Integrative Nutrition followed by a BA in Health Arts & Sciences from Goddard College. Pamala is currently pursuing a Master's degree in nutrition education from Hawthorn University.

Pamala's studies have led her to conclude that healthy lifestyles begin at home. As a bonus to her real estate clients, Pamala teaches them how to live healthier lives starting in their own kitchen. Exposure to potentially harmful toxins and chemicals can be minimized by a process she calls "greening". In addition, she works with a professional designer to create a family vegetable garden.

When not working, Pamala can be found volunteering in one of the civic or humanitarian originations she supports, traveling to a car show with her husband, tie-dying t-shirts with a grandchild or whipping up a delish plant-based meal for anyone that's hungry.

pamalasmith@kw.com
(707)580-7517
www.pamalasmith.kwrealty.com
www.healthyhomeagent.com

STRONG AND INDEPENDENT WOMEN, A LEGACY
By: Kerry Hargraves

When I think of my grandmother, Nana, I see her dressed in grey slacks, a starched, brilliantly white, collared shirt and red blazer. I'm sure she wore other clothes but this was her iconic look. With her close-cut white hair, distinctive nose (the result of an unset break as a young woman), ready smile and twinkling blue eyes, she was a popular figure strolling along Park Blvd. with her tiny silver poodle.

Nana lived alone in a studio apartment tucked way up in the back corner of an old apartment building. It was a steep climb up the brick stairs to the porch she shared with one neighbor. The black wrought iron railing was almost always engulfed in a lush honeysuckle vine. She is the one who taught me the secret to capturing the sweet drop of nectar within the blossoms. The sight or scent of honeysuckle evokes her spirit for me even today.

I spent many weekends in that tiny apartment. In the early years, we shared an old-fashioned sleeper couch. She would lift the seat and with a magical click the whole couch would lay out flat – well, sort of flat. The horsehair upholstery was scratchy through the sheets we put on every night and put away every morning as the room was transformed from sleep mode to living mode.

Eventually the magic couch was replaced by a fold-out sofa bed. We traded scratchy for the metal bar. If you've ever slept on an older convertible sofa you know exactly what I mean. Open it almost filled the room, so furniture had to be moved and the couch cushions stacked just so for there to be space, and to be able to squeeze around it.

Next door was a restaurant and bar. Saturday night's Nana would make sure I was fed and tucked into bed and head down her rickety wooden back steps. From the back yard, she could walk directly into the bar. When the weather was warm enough she kept the back door to the apartment open so I could hear the music and laughter. I wasn't afraid of the dark, but silence made me anxious.

In true grandmotherly fashion, she spoiled me. Most weekends she served me breakfast in bed, peanut butter and bacon on toast. This is still one of my favorites. It was accompanied by my cup of "coffee." Of course, it was milk with just a splash of coffee but I always felt so sophisticated.

During the holiday season, we'd make eggnog from scratch. Working together in her little kitchen, whisking the eggs and milk with a hand cranked egg beater, adding just the right amount of cinnamon, and laughing as my egg beater skills made droplets of the foamy mixture fly. She would add dollop of rum extract to make my cup of eggnog just like the grownups drank theirs.

Nana, Peggie to her friends, had a best friend and running mate. A diminutive woman, Inez probably stood maybe 4'8" on her tip-toes. As a little kid, I remember wanting to grow to be as tall as Inez. I suppose I was setting an achievable goal.

They met at work. They both worked at Convair; a company that manufactured military aircraft. Nana was a sheet former. She manhandled large sheets of steel in and out of even larger stamping presses. This was in the days before OSHA and the constant noise robbed her of much of her hearing. I don't remember what Inez's job was. I do remember their conversations about the SOB bosses. I wish I could say that women in the work place no longer have the same complaints, but alas, even though it has improved, the things they griped about then are still being griped about today.

They would go out after work, have a few cocktails, a little dinner, maybe another cocktail or two. One night, driving home they ended up on the runway at Lindbergh Field. Apparently, Inez confused the light at the seaplane crossing for the turn on to W Laurel Dr. The gate was open and in they drove. Luckily, it was late enough that no flights were arriving or departing. They gave airport security a merry chase. They loved this story and it got better and more outrageous with every telling.

I'm sure there was talk; two unmarried women, working in an airplane factory, wearing slacks, frequenting bars, laughing loud, enjoying life and not giving a damn about what anyone else though about it.

I don't recall either of them ever mentioning a date, or men they met. I know Nana was done with men. Her father took her out of school in 3rd grade and made her go to work. As an intelligent woman who loved to learn and had great curiosity this left her with a deep and lingering resentment. She was an avid reader, but her lack of formal education remained a sore spot all her life.

I mentioned at the beginning of this story that Nana had a distinctive nose. Her story was that she broke it running into a door. I never thought to question that story until she was gone.

Putting together bits and pieces of what I know, I'm pretty sure that either her father or her husband was responsible.

I never met her husband, my grandfather. I do know she hated him with a passion. How or why she ended up married to a man she despised I never know. She bore 3 children with him; the first 2 were sons and then later a daughter, my mother. The daughter was the apple of her father's eye. They formed a bond that excluded Nana. This influenced the mother-daughter relationship and created a breach never healed.

In 1946, my mother moved from New Jersey to San Diego where my father was stationed in the Navy. Nana came with her. I assume her husband had died since good Catholic women didn't divorce.

This is when she found the little apartment that would become her home for the next 40 years. Her life was her own. She found work, friends, and books. The grocery store, liquor store, Catholic Church, and a movie theater were within walking distance. The beauty salon and the Chinese laundry were close by, and of course next door was The Flame, the restaurant and bar whose music and laughter I could hear as I snuggled under the covers in her tiny apartment. For those few places that weren't within walking distance there was the Number 7 bus.

That bus took us to the park, the zoo, and my favorite place, the carousel. Starting at around 8 years old I would ride the bus alone to get to Nana's place for the weekend rather than wait for my mother to be able to drive me. Her independence and self-sufficient ways were rubbing off on me already.

I remember a picture of the Pope hung in her dressing room until he was replaced by JFK. By then she had stopped making me take the walk to the church every Sunday.

In her early 60's Nana had a serious heart attack. After a short stay in the hospital she was back at home and refusing help. I'm sure the years of trips up and down that steep flight of stairs to her apartment helped her be as healthy as she was. The heart attack changed only one thing – she stopped smoking! Other than that, life continued as it always had.

Several years later she was diagnosed with breast cancer. In those days, the only treatment was radical mastectomy. She lost one breast and for a time, she also lost her independence. That was the greater loss in her mind.

Her time recuperating in her daughter's (my mother's) home was a strain on them both. In ordinary circumstances, they were seldom able to spend more than 24 hours together without a significant blow-up. Adding the ingredients of worry, weakness, and helplessness didn't improve their relationship. Nana wanted nothing more than to get back to her own place, to be left alone, to do as she pleased. My mother wanted to be helpful. To be honest, she wasn't very good at it. Nursing was not one of her strong suits. Neither was empathy. Two strong willed, determined, independent women, each trying desperately to get their own way, it was a hostile brew.

I hated the yelling, slamming doors, and angry silences. To avoid being pulled into the middle and pressured to take sides I buried myself in books. This is still how I handle conflict.

Once Nana returned home they spent less and less time with one another. Holidays were the exception. My mother loved to entertain. She would pull together a big spread, invite her friends and select neighborhood strays to her holiday open house.

This is one memory about these holidays that never fails to make me laugh, and one that drove my mother nuts. We would go get Nana the day before the holiday so we could spend a day together before that party. (You would think they'd learn.) My mother would spend the day doing as much food prep as she could. Nana would try to help, get drunk and have to go to bed early. Since she went to bed before the sun went down, Nana would be up first. Just about the time the rest of the household was stirring she would start making the gravy. It never failed that a generous portion of that gravy would get spilled down the front of the stove.

It maybe a little weird that this is one of my favorite holiday memories, but I can still see Nana in her housecoat, ladle in hand, drink by her side, and gravy dripping down the oven door, trying to do her part for the holiday meal. Every year!

Of course, it wouldn't be the gravy my mother wanted and it wouldn't be on the schedule my mother wanted, and the mess! (Did I mention my mother was a clean freak?) This is when the traditional holiday fight would begin.

Eventually the strain between them became so great that they severed all relations.

Many of their problems stemmed from their similarities. They shared a fierce independence, strong opinions and an unwillingness to compromise. I'd like to think I inherited the independence and not the unwillingness to compromise but I'm not so sure. I suspect I'm just subtler about making sure I get my own way.

My mother, unlike her mother, loved men. She had a weakness for the bad boys, (a trait I inherited) and in fact, married 3 of them. My father, who got her out of New Jersey and to California and gave her 2 babies. My sister, born 4 years before me, died at age 2 of Cystic Fibrosis. This, I believe, was the genesis of my mother's clean freak streak. My speculation on what ended that first marriage is that the Navy kept him away from home too much.

My mother was a woman who needed attention.

Her second husband filled that gap. Perhaps too well; it's a fine line between attention and control, and he crossed it. When I was 8, we snuck our few belongings and a little furniture out of the house and move into an apartment without him. For a while, she wouldn't answer the door at night and checked under the hood for a bomb before she started her car in the mornings.

After a couple of years, she married for the last time. The appeal, I think, was the perks of his profession. Marty was a wholesale liquor salesman and was welcomed in all the best restaurants and bars, invited to fabulous parties, and had exciting and fun friends. Once she got him home though she discovered that he wasn't as fun and glittery as he appeared. It lasted 2 years. She kept several of his friends though.

Like Nana, after her experiments with matrimony my mother settled into a great apartment in a community she loved. Made friends and became a bit of a local celebrity. Eventually she became the manager of her apartment building. Imagine an only slightly less bohemian version of Anna Madrigal managing 28 Barbary Lane in Armistead Maupin's **_Tales of the City._**

She continued to work, to hang out at her favorite watering holes, laugh with her friends, and insist on her independence right up until she succumbed to pancreatic cancer at the too young age of 62. She used to tell me that she didn't want to put me through what she went through with her mother. I believe that's why she died so young.

In mid-life, my grandmother and my mother both had the courage to craft lives that were uniquely their own. They shed the traditional roles society assigned to them and embraced their independence. Neither of them gave a damn about what anyone else thought their choices.

I inherited the strong, independent spirit that ran through their veins; as did my daughter, Marilyn. I tell her that she comes from a long line of women to be reckoned with; women who have found their own way, on their own terms. Women who don't give a damn about what anybody else thinks about it. I am proud and delighted that Marilyn is carrying on the family tradition. We're lucky. This way of being is natural to us. It's our legacy.

So many women get caught up in the roles they play, not realizing (or ignoring) what truly makes them happy. I am a wife, mother to a human daughter and 2 fur babies, a retired business owner, recovering corporate executive, artist, lover of great cocktails, craft-a-holic, Arizona resident, and a whole lot of other roles that, quite frankly, don't begin to define the whole me.

Can I tell you a secret?

Your roles, past awards, and the things you do for others are not the sum of your happiness. That comes from you; the real, deep, dark, and even absurdly silly things that bring you joy. I've met one too many miserable old biddies that have lost their way as their titles and roles shift.

What about you? Do you know who you are behind your assigned roles? Are you living life on your own terms? You can, you know.

It takes a little bit of courage and a willingness to change. Yes, change is scary. Your friends, family, colleagues don't want you change. That will disturb their world. You won't be playing your role, staying in character. Even scarier, if you change they might have to change as well.

But it's YOUR life. Your one, singular, magical, magnificent life and you owe it to yourself, and to the generations of women who will come after you to live that life as fully, joyfully, and uniquely as you can.

It seems like a huge undertaking but like all journeys, it begins with one small step. That first step: change one thing. It doesn't have to be big or complex, but you must commit to it. For example: change the color of your hair, or switch from contact lenses to glasses. Do something like this and I can pretty much guarantee you, in a year you'll look back in amazement at the transformations that have taken place.

Learn to ignore what other people think about your changes, about how you live. Remember their judgments say more about them than about you; this includes the little voice in your head, I call her "The Nag." Fire her. She won't stay fired, but just keep on firing her. She will eventually retire to the background.

Find things that make you happy and bring more of them into your day to day. Allow yourself the freedom to explore new things, obey the impulse. When you get tired of something or it no longer brings you joy, stop doing it. No need to explain.

Laugh! Laugh loud and often. Look for people who make you laugh and hang out with them

Don't wait until the children are grown, or you retire. Don't wait until you've lost that last 10 pounds, or had your knee replaced. Don't wait until you have more money or fewer responsibilities. Start now.

What will be your legacy?

Kerry Hargraves is a creative, intuitive, sparkly explorer. She walks, sometimes skips, along the playful path.

At any given moment, you may find her blowing bubbles in an elevator, spreading her wings and flying around corners on the street, singing loud in her car, or dancing to the grocery store music. She will be spreading smiles, creating laughter, and encouraging others to join in the fun.

After a long career as a manufacturing executive and consultant, she gave it all up for a flock of pink plastic flamingos. She spent 16 years delivering surprises in the middle of the night, helping mischievous people delight their friends and family. There was also a 5-year stint as a custom sign maker. This gave her the opportunity to indulge her love of all things creative and mechanical. Saws, drills, paint sprayers, vinyl cutters, gold leaf, and of course a little splash of paint on every article of clothing she owned.

Kerry currently fills her time providing computer administrative support to a few select clients. She paints, coils baskets, and is learning pottery. In her spare time, she teaches programs that help women discover and embrace their bold, fun, brave, vibrant Bodacious Bad-ass Old Broad and unleash her on the world. This helps the world becomes a brighter, happier place. Who isn't all in for that!?

After a million jobs* in about 50 years chances are Kerry has been there or done that. And she has the refrigerator magnet collection to prove it. Along the way, she learned the power of a playful spirit for changing lives, changing the world, and improving every aspect of life.

*Only a slight exaggeration
https://www.KerryHargraves.com
https://www.facebook.com/kerry.hargraves
https://www.linkedin.com/in/kerryhargraves/
https://www.pinterest.com/kerrylim/
https://www.instagram.com/kerryhargraves/
https://plus.google.com/u/0/+KerryHargraves

Legacies of Great Joy and Love

STIRRING UP LOVE
By: Mary E. Knippel

"Miracles occur naturally as expressions of love...everything that comes from love is a miracle."
Marianne Williamson

Some children associate Grandma with lilac water, rose bushes, or elegant dining. When I think of mine, I smell biscuits fresh from the oven, hear bacon frying and popping in the black cast iron pan, and see a crisply ironed flowered apron accented with rick rack covering her shirtwaist dress, and see her black sensible shoes.

My mother's mother was the embodiment of unconditional love. She didn't judge or discipline...she just loved. My grandmother believed everything could be made better with a cookie.

It's true that all of us are not destined to have our names written down in the history books. I believe it is also true that God has designed all of us with a specific purpose in life and we will be remembered for how we did or didn't live in pursuit of that purpose. Our lives are all individual threads woven together into the universal story. Think of the world as over 7 billion threads creating a beautiful and colorful rich tapestry.

Grandma made you feel special. She remembered who liked what and made a fuss about giving everybody his or her specific preference. A hug from Grandma meant you got enveloped in those ample arms and felt like being wrapped in a warm cocoon.

Grandma manifested Miracles in her own way. Her meals were not so sophisticated, but she loved to bake. She was creative in her own way. Everyone has memories of doing something special with their grandmother. She was a constant in my early childhood. In fact, we lived under the same roof until I was 8.

I don't remember her ever reading to us, but I do have a vivid memory of enjoying a particular kind of story with her. We lived close enough that I'd come home from school for lunch. I would rush home so that I could join Grandma for the last few minutes watching her 'story' as she called her soap opera. I was sad when As the World Turns went off the air. It was a part of a legacy I shared with her. She loved her stories. Watching her story was the only time I really saw her sitting down.

She may not have been very tall or outspoken, yet she had a powerful presence in our lives. We always knew we could count on Grandma's undivided attention. No matter what she was doing around the house, from cooking or baking to ironing or washing, she'd stop what she was doing to listen to her grandchildren's stories about anything and everything from clouds to clowns. She let us know we were important and we mattered. Because she showed us our life mattered, I believe that's what made her life matter. She knew that we needed her care and affection from her. She loved being needed. She showed me it was okay to be express your emotions and especially to someone who had a sympathetic ear. Everyone deserves to be nurtured in such a sweet way. Everyone needs to know that their life matters.

Her life mattered.
Your life matters.
Yes, you are only one person and that's all it takes when you are living on purpose.

Think about the solitary lives that have impacted the entire world in some form for generations. Some names stand out like Jesus, Mother Teresa, or Gandhi. There are also countless world leaders, poets, scholars, scientists, artists and many, many more who have made contributions by living their purpose whom we will never know. That doesn't make what they did matter any less.

Every life matters!
Our individual stories matter. You matter!

Each and every one of us is hungry to be seen and heard. Our fondest desire is to know that another human being acknowledges and respects us as another person living on purpose. Each of us has a distinct purpose in life. The sum of all or our experiences and how we cope with every experience factor into the human being we are now, are becoming, and will become. Every day we have the opportunity to have an impact…on ourselves, on the immediate people around us, and on the people, we don't even know yet how we are influencing.

Be genuine and sincere in your interaction with everyone. When you say: "Hello, how are you today?" stop and listen to the response. Remember to be polite and always say please and thank you. Consider going beyond the golden rule to treat others the way you want to be treated. What about treating others with unconditional love?

When I think of home, so many memories come flooding forward like the coming attractions at the movies, except these scenes all took place years ago. Ordinary scenes because it's just people gathered around the kitchen table eating breakfast, lunch or supper. Yet, they are extraordinary because we were generations of a family gathered together around a too small Formica table and eating on worn Melmac plates, enjoying crisp bacon sandwiches made with homemade biscuits. Grandma passing a plate of freshly baked chocolate chip cookies as we are eating and laughing sharing stories and jokes, being nurtured body and soul around the table. Grandma always dished up plenty of love to go with whatever scrapes caused tears.

Making dinner matters whether it's for a family of four, or just you, nurturing your body is right up there with nurturing your soul; washing the laundry matters, listening to the stories behind little tears matters.

I remember standing at our tiny kitchen window watching the kids playing at the elementary school across the railroad tracks and wanting to be over there too. Grandma would scoop me up her ample arms and give me a hug, then shake her head and tell me that my time would come soon enough. I was about 5-years-old and happy to be right there with her in the kitchen watching her frying, mixing, baking and stirring things up!

When I was 10-years-old, my cousin (also 10) and I went to visit my aunt, Grandma's youngest daughter. Grandma went too. We all stayed in her little apartment for a week. The apartment was really one large room with a small kitchen. I remember the sink and refrigerator took up one wall and the stove was behind the door so you had to be careful coming in and out not to get burned by what was cooking on the stove. There wasn't a kitchen table so my cousin and I balanced our plates on our laps and sat on the floor picnic style. My aunt had a hide-a-bed couch, desk, 2 chairs and chest of drawers. The shared bathroom was down the hall. Everything was in easy to reach distance in the kitchen, which was great for someone living alone. Not so great when you have houseguests and two of them are obnoxious pre-teens and your mother.

The kitchen was tiny but mighty with all the gadgets and accessories my aunt could afford on an office worker's salary. She wanted to show off for her mother and her adoring nieces. My family loved to eat. My aunt loved to cook and entertain.
Grandma excelled at making treats. Baking was her thing. I think that's where my mother got her love of baking. I think that's where I get my love of nurturing from the two of them. Grandma dished up unconditional love with anything she served. In this matchbox of a kitchen, Grandma created a Martha Stewart worthy 6-layer cake complete with boiled icing. It wasn't any grand occasion, other than the fact that she wanted to make a nice meal for us. It was an act of love. She'd say, "Oh, I like to keep busy." She was busy all the time. Cooking, baking, doing the laundry, washing the dishes, that's how she showed she loved us. That's how she showed we mattered to her. Small in stature, she towered over everyone with compassion and inspiring good in others. She was pure love.

She demonstrated then what I continue today; doing the little things that have a big impact, on those around me. Small gestures like remembering what type of dental floss to buy, green apples not red, hot -pepper cheese not American, and the like. Paying attention to the details that make life rich and demonstrates you matter to me.

The worst scolding, we kids ever got was "Kitty, Kitty, Kitty." Meaning you children are fighting and need to share like the little kitties do, all drinking from the same dish.

Grandma always had a welcoming smile and a Honey, I'm so glad you're here expression on her face. A legacy I seek to bring forward too. I think a part of Grandma's legacy I will always treasure is her faith. She didn't venture far from her front door. Her world revolved around the kitchen, the clothesline in the backyard, occasionally the beauty shop up town and, of course, church a half a block from our back door. We went to the local parochial school and daily Mass was part of our routine. Mass was part of Grandma's routine several times a week and it was a treat to have her smiling at us as we filed past to take our places with our classmates.

Grandma had hardships, but accepted them all with grace and prayer. She thought she was going through the change of life only to discover she was pregnant at the same time as her oldest daughter! Her husband was plagued with health problems and died in his sleep. Grandma's attitude was to be grateful and patient. God always had a plan. God was a loving God. Through it all she never complained and looked for the good in every situation.
Although she never ventured away from home much, Grandma gambled. She played Bingo! Sometimes on Sunday afternoons the Ladies Church Unit would hold a Bingo fundraiser. It was fun and inexpensive Sunday afternoon entertainment and a chance to show off dessert making skills on the refreshment table.

Grandma always had time for us children. She was patient and she was unendingly kind. I know it irritated others that she never got mad. She accepted what happened and found the good in everyone and everything. I guess she was Pollyanna playing the Glad Game before Disney had ever optioned the rights to the movie.

When my relatives got together for the occasional gatherings, they would outdo each other with new recipes and putting out the prettiest dishes and linens. A family favorite arrived at one such occasion; for as long as I can remember recipes have acquired names in my Mother's cookbook with the Christian names of their originator. Take Madonna Bars for example. The first time I took Madonna bars anywhere I think I was a young secretary at Sperry Univac. It seemed to me that the guys in my group had never had anything homemade. I know I'm dating myself to say that this was about the time that Madonna was making a name for herself so when people asked the name of the bars and who brought them their eyebrows shot up when I innocently said, "I brought them and we call them Madonna Bars."

In many families Madonna is a very old, common name. Contrasting the famous Madonna and the person who introduced this dessert recipe to our family circle is like comparing a complicated baked Alaska to Rice Krispy treats. Our Madonna had characteristics very similar to her mother and her sisters, including my grandmother who was one of those sisters. These women were homebodies; devoted to family and absolutely loved to bake.

All the women in my family like to bake and are always trying out new recipes. We all fell in love with the richness and simplicity of the bars and everyone was soon adept at making the bar. It's so simple a child can do it. You don't need a recipe really. Just melt a stick of butter. Add a cup or so of crushed graham cracker crumbs, enough so that all the butter is absorbed. Top that with about a cup of shredded coconut, a cup of chocolate chips and some chopped nuts if you like. Some people like to add chopped walnuts, butterscotch chips or peanut butter chips for variety. Then you cover the whole thing with the entire contents of a can of Eagle Brand Condensed Milk. Bake at 350° for about 25-30 minutes until the edges are a golden brown and bubbly. They are called a variety of things in all the women's magazine and have been around for years. Some people call them Magic Cookie Bars. Other times they are known as 7-Layer Bars. But in my family and everyone close to me and for generations since then - they are Madonna Bars.

Dear Reader, through these pages the message I invite you to take away is that the little things do matter. I understand that it's hard to remember to stop for the little things in this fast-paced world. At the same time, it's vitally important that you do.

Life is in the details. Pay attention to all the little things that make life worth living. Like those distinctive creature comforts in everything from food to music, theatre to sports, city living or country life. The details such as knowing the preferences: creamy or chunky peanut butter, dark or milk chocolate, peas or carrots, mayo or mustard, classical or jazz, city apartment or cottage in the suburbs. Yes, it's wonderful if someone remembers your birthday and sends you a card.

That's an annual mark it on the calendar kind of thoughtfulness. I'm suggesting the everyday kind of details; like someone observing that you prefer tea to coffee. When was the last time somebody knew what type of tea you drink? Taking notice and remembering those little things has a big impact and makes a lasting impression. Life is too short not to explore and be adventurous in little ways in some form. Try a new recipe. Change your hairstyle. Take a class. Listen to a new type of music. Grandma's spirit of unconditional love lives on in me and I hope I've passed it on to my daughter.

Now you have all the ingredients to perform your own brand of magic. Love is in the details! Go stir up some unconditional love in your life for yourself and others.

About the Author

Best-selling author Mary E. Knippel, Writer Unleashed at YourWritingMentor.com, publisher at Authentic Grace Publishing and inspirational speaker, is fiercely committed to guiding you to unleash your story worth writing. With a firm philosophy that *No one can tell your story but YOU*, Mary invites you to take pen in hand to deliver your expertise to the world. Using her 30 years as a journalist, and the power of storytelling, she is on a mission to support you to be visible, vibrant and prosperous. Someone is waiting to hear your story…the story only you can tell.

As a journal writer since the age of 11, Mary knows the enormous power and healing capabilities of the written word. A two-time breast cancer survivor she used writing and other creative tools in her recovery and chronicles the results in her upcoming book, *The Secret Artist*, where she shares what she has learned to help you move from survive to thrive. Learn more about Mary's virtual classes and workshops, receive free writing tips and techniques as well as what to do about writer's block, or invite her to speak to your group, by visiting her website at www.yourwritingmentor.com.

http://yourwritingmentor.com
http://facebook.com/maryeknippel.author
650-440-5616

CHILDHOOD SAFE HAVENS: GRANDMA ROSE & EXPRESSIVE ART
By: Trina Swerdlow

I'm alone, sitting cross-legged on the floor in my dimly lit bedroom. I dump all of my crayons out of their box and watch them roll onto the floor. I smile and breathe in the waxy smell of these colorful "magical sticks." A stack of paper is perched in front of me.

First, I draw a black fuzzy dog that looks like Duchess, our neighbor's blind Cocker Spaniel. Duchess is a sweet girl! While drawing, I think about petting her soft, wavy fur. I giggle and set her aside.

On a new piece of paper, I draw a great big lady holding a heart. I add a tree and some clouds in the sky. Then, with the bright red crayon, I slowly draw roses all over the lady's pretty dress.

~ * ~ * ~ * ~

Art has always been a safe haven for me. As a small child, I often disappeared into crayon and paper imaginary worlds. I especially loved cutting my characters out. Doing this brought them to life, kind of like using a magic wand! I remember playfully animating my character's movements and talking to them.

I connected deeply to these "paper people" because they felt safe.

Sadly, I was raised in a dangerous home where I experienced violence and childhood sexual abuse. My ability to create art shielded me from the brutal reality of my home life and gave me a sense of power. These imaginary worlds were safe havens where I could hide amidst the bright colors and images.

In response to the dangerous environment, my mind-body tried to protect me by releasing loads of stress hormones: adrenaline and cortisol. Living with high levels of these hormones, wreaked havoc on my body and resulted in chronic digestive problems, including irritable bowel syndrome. Feeling relaxed and safe wasn't a state that I embraced often…*unless I was at Grandma's house.*

Grandma Rose's Soul Food

My Grandma Rose was the only unconditionally loving, adult family member in my childhood. I saw her a few times a month and being with her was soul food for me. **Grandma Rose was my rock.** Whenever I looked into her big brown eyes, I knew I could do no wrong.

Not only did Grandma Rose nourish my soul—she nourished my aching belly with her cooking. Surprisingly, my challenged digestive system quieted down to receive grandma's healing matzo ball soup, beet borscht, and cinnamon bread with plump golden raisins. The sweet smell of the baking bread filled Grandma's kitchen and then danced throughout the rest of her house.

Another fond memory I have is when Grandma Rose would take me into her arms, look deeply into my eyes, and rock me while singing:

"Que Sera, Sera,
Whatever will be, will be
The future's not ours, to see
Que Sera, Sera..." *

*Ahh...*my "rock" was rocking me.

Even though Grandma Rose didn't see what was going on in my home life and rescue me from it, I am deeply grateful to have had her love.

In addition to my art, Grandma was truly my other safe haven.

* Song: "Que Sera, Sera" © 1955 Jay Livingston, Ray Evans

Discovering a Creative Tribe

As the years went by, my creativity continued to flourish. In my teens, my art became more sophisticated as far as technique and skill however the subject matter was often dark with frightening, gory imagery.

During this time, I exhibited my surreal paintings in a fine art show. The other artists were sharing their art featuring beautiful flowers and colorful landscapes. At one point in the day, a silver-haired woman walked up and stared nervously at my art. She looked bewildered. Her gaze flipped back and forth between my art and me.

"You painted these?" the lady said with a quiver in her voice. *"But you look like such a sweet girl."*

I had yet to link my creative expression to my traumatic childhood. Even with my surreal style, I received an art scholarship from a junior college in Phoenix, Arizona. Later, in my twenties, I attended Art Center College of Design in Pasadena, California. I loved being in this "melting pot" with talented artists from all over the world.

I found my creative tribe!

Four years later, I was proud to receive my Bachelor in Fine Arts in Illustration. However, I remember one of my instructors telling me that in order to make a living I'd probably have to move to New York where there was a market for "tormented-looking" editorial art. I was not happy hearing this bewildering feedback.

My Creative Career Unfolds

After finishing college, I stayed in Southern California and freelanced. Unfortunately, finding suitable assignments for my "style" wasn't easy, but I managed to illustrate some magazine articles, posters, and a few advertisements for various products. I tamed my surreal style as much as possible to get work.

Thankfully, I was hired for a large freelance project. Richard Saul Wurman (who would become the creator of TED Conferences) hired me to illustrate one of his travel guidebooks—the first edition of **Hawaii Access**. This large freelance project was an exciting introduction into the book-publishing world. And, because I only illustrated "things" (shells, flower leis, and topographical maps) my surreal art style was easily kept at bay.

After the book was finished, I found a full-time dream job.

I became an Art Director/Designer of greeting cards and gift products. The publisher moved me from Southern California to Northern California, where I built an art department from scratch. My hard work and love of art was paying off!

As an Art Director/Designer of photography greeting cards, the torment that often crept in when I drew illustrated characters didn't have an opportunity to express itself. Instead, I hired adorable animals like puppies (including my Sealyham Terrier named Argyle), kittens, and a variety of other precious creatures—to be photographed for greeting cards.

Next, I created a teddy bear character, Val Bear, who became an international hit. Val Bear was a handmade stuffed animal that appeared on posters, calendars, puzzles, and hundreds of greeting cards.

I was in my creative zone creating Val Bear's quirky personality and designing her clothes. *(Much like the cut-out "paper friends" I created as a child).*

Our customers were thrilled with our products and my career was skyrocketing.

From the outside, my life and career looked fabulous. However, the inside view was a totally different story. Every day, I experienced high levels of anxiety. In addition, I still suffered with serious digestive challenges that required buying Pepto Bismol® in the super-sized bottle and I often struggled with frightening dreams while I slept. *(Unknown to me these issues were all symptoms of my childhood trauma-induced PTSD: Post-Traumatic Stress Disorder.)*

A Terrifying "Wake-up Call"

Driving to work one morning, I got a "wake-up call" while I was crossing a Bay Area bridge. The driver behind me failed to notice that all of the cars in front of him had completely stopped on the bridge.

~*~ *~ *~

I hear an ear-piercing squeal from a car's slammed-on brakes. I tense up. The car behind me violently smashes into my brand-new Volkswagen Jetta. The crashing sounds escalate as the domino effect continues. **The result is a massive multi-car pile-up.** *Due to the wreckage on this narrow bridge, no emergency vehicles could get to any of us (for what seemed like hours). While waiting for help, I feel frozen and trapped. I try not to fixate on the turbulent ocean swirling far below me.*

~*~ *~ *~

In addition to a neck injury, I experienced aftershocks of heightened PTSD. When my symptoms worsened each week, I visited a psychologist. During the initial sessions, I learned relaxation and cognitive exercises designed to help quiet down my hypervigilant nervous system.

Within a couple of months of seeing this psychologist, repressed memories of childhood sexual abuse came up to heal. My unconscious knew that this therapist would act as a "healing container" to make it *safe* for me to remember what I'd lived through as a child.

Thankfully, I was no longer alone, trapped in the isolation of my forgotten traumas. At last, I had a caring professional to shine light on the fragmented puzzle pieces of my early life.

It quickly became apparent that long before the bridge accident, as a result of the recurring traumas I experienced as a child, my nervous system became locked in the stress response—the "fight-flight-freeze" reaction.

After I remembered the first large chunk of traumatic memories and shared them with my therapist, I was gifted with a "new" digestive system.

Unbelievable relief!

All of the chronic stomach and bowel symptoms were gone. I no longer unconsciously held enormous tension in my gut, which was pushing down the overwhelming childhood memories. Thankfully, in addition to offering periods of respite, my art expressions gave me an outlet to share my bottled-up emotions. For example, at five years old, I created a crayon drawing of a clown. This drawing clearly illustrated **the fear that I felt in my life and in my body**, at that young age.

Experiencing this healing transformation, made me in awe of the profound connection between the unconscious mind and the body!

And, not only did I access peacefulness in my body, but the torment that had relentlessly expressed through my artwork—disappeared. From then on, whenever I looked at my past artwork, I clearly SAW the torment.

Miraculously, I could then express my internal JOY through my paintings!

To see this creative transformation, meet my playful "alter ego" here.

Stepping On to a New Path

A few years into my continued personal growth journey I started working with a new mentor; a clinical hypnotherapist. During my rich work using inspiring hypnotherapy tools, **I reconnected with how important Grandma Rose was to me as a child. I got in**

touch with how much of grandma's unconditional love, I still held in my heart.

Unfortunately, Grandma passed away when I was a teenager. So, by the time I realized Grandma Rose's profound contributions to my survival, it was too late to share my deepest gratitude with her.

That's when I decided to make an **art doll** to honor her. In a local craft store, I found a pre-sewn canvas doll. I painted Rose's portrait on the face, then added ears and earrings. Next, I attached silver doll hair and created a teensy-weensy braid for the top of the head.

I decorated the beige canvas dress with large red roses and loving words of gratitude.

Sharing Sacred Gifts

In 2002, a *still small voice* from deep inside myself was getting louder and louder. I wanted to change my career and help others. That's when I gathered my courage and took a leap of faith.

I downsized my design work in the publishing world to go back to school and become a certified clinical hypnotherapist. In 2005

I opened my private practice. A few months later, my new business was flourishing.

Within the first year, a book I authored/illustrated, **Stress Reduction Journal** was published. A few years later, I had a monthly column, "Transformations" in *Alive* magazine.

Now, twelve years later, I still *love* my purpose-driven work and I've added a holistic weight loss program that I created called **Weight Loss 18 Minutes**. This program connects with the mind-body-spirit and offers guided imagery to help people nourish their hungry hearts.

Meanwhile, I continue to offer general stress management tools and work with adult survivors of childhood trauma. I love teaching clients how to create safe havens inside themselves, to serve as strong foundations for deeper healing work—such as releasing shame and embracing self-love.

During my own personal growth process, I discovered that the healthy "Wise Woman" in me could soothe/heal my wounded "Inner Child" ***by taking myself into my own arms***.

Thank you, Grandma Rose,
*I have shared your
precious legacy*
and taught many dear souls
how to create an internal

~ Safe Haven ~
and lovingly
take themselves…
into their own arms.

Three Transformational Tools
to Honor Safe Havens

Now, if you feel inspired to honor your own life-affirming resources, then I have three tools to share:

1. Think about and affirm…

- Who or what outer positive resources during your childhood ** offered you love, comfort, or safety? *(Pets count!)* Consider honoring these **safe havens** by framing photos that will remind you of these precious roots.
- Who or what outer positive resources in your current life offer you love and comfort? ***Do you reciprocate and offer gratitude?***

2. Embrace creative expression each week. Be it art, gardening, sewing, theatre, healthy cooking, flower arranging, dancing, singing, or playing a musical instrument.

3. Offer yourself nurturing, positive affirmations each day to continually *cultivate self-love.*

Let's stay connected. Visit my website to sign-up for my free Transformational TIPS Newsletter and receive an inspiring poster:
www.TrinaSwerdlow.com

* Song: "Que Sera, Sera" © 1955 Jay Livingston, Ray Evans

** If you had a painful childhood that is negatively impacting your current life, seek professional support from a compassionate therapist or a skilled spiritual counselor.

About the Author

Trina Swerdlow, BFA, CCHT

Trina Swerdlow is a Transformational Thought Leader who has spoken on stages throughout the San Francisco Bay Area and is the Author of ***Stress Reduction Journal: Meditate & Journal Your Way to Better Health.***

Trina is an Artist, a nondenominational Minister, and a Certified Clinical Hypnotherapist with a private practice in Danville, California.

Trina's artwork and biography were honored in the book: ***Outstanding American Illustrators Today 2.***

Born in Phoenix, Arizona, as a small child Trina often disappeared into imaginary worlds that she created with crayons and paper.

Her ability to create art helped her survive the brutal reality of her home life—where she experienced violence and childhood sexual abuse.

At 29 years old, Trina stepped onto a healing path. Decades later, she left a successful career as an art director and greeting card designer **to begin her most important work...*helping others*.**

She then became a certified clinical hypnotherapist in private practice. Now, more than twelve years later, Trina teaches clients (including adult sexual abuse survivors) how to create *safe havens* inside themselves so they can release shame and embrace self-love.

Trina's newest creation, **Weight Loss 18 Minutes** is a program that teaches people how to transform *emotional eating* into *mindful eating*. This holistic program offers inspiring guided imagery to empower people to nourish their hungry hearts *and move toward their healthy goals.*

It's my privilege
to offer ***Transformational Tools***
that empower people
to find their voices,
take back their
precious bodies
and reclaim
~ *JOY* ~

Learn More…

(925) 285-5759

www.TrinaSwerdlow.com

www.WeightLoss18Minutes.com

https://www.facebook.com/Trina-Swerdlow-BFA-CCHT-1510660185834391/

https://www.linkedin.com/in/trina-swerdlow-822aa24/

@TrinaSwerdlow

WISDOM OF LIFE WITH GRANDMA NETTIE
By: Angela Blaha

LOVE

The day you stop learning is the day you die." Was my Grandmother's response after she heard me express a big sigh, as I tried to understand English Literature. Her words compelled me to learn, even when I was a frustrated teenager buried in homework. Her ideas ignited my thirst for knowledge, my endless quest for information, and my need to understand. It was as if she could see into some level of my being which was not visible to the eye.

She reveled in even the most trivial of knowledge, as she would sit at the dining room table doing crossword puzzles from the daily paper. I remember her shouting out the words with such a passion, as if there was a prize to be won; but for Grandma Nettie, knowledge was the prize and her exuberance was another function of her love of learning.

She was a pioneer in her quest for learning and attended college and played basketball. She always amazed and inspired me as I longed to follow in her footprint. She was a simple woman who was passionate about life, family, learning and her ability to 'just know things.'

Her passion for the simple things in life was something that intrigued me, I grew up in poverty and her take on societal quest for "stuff" was that they were looking in the wrong direction for happiness in life. She listened carefully to your every word as she was very passionate about making you feel heard and seen. She understood me in a way I never understood myself. And she loved me in a way no one else has.

Her deep, blue eyes, like two oceans on her face, bore right into me, seeing deep into my soul, seeing me in a way no one else ever did. Every time my grandma Nettie looked at me, she looked beyond the surface, really, she let me know how much she loved me without saying a word. The love I received from her was unlike anything in the human experience, it was deeper than humanity. She loved me with an intensity that was as powerful as it was unconditioned. She taught me about the power of pure love.

Love was her whole life; life just wasn't worthwhile to her if she didn't love every moment of it. I don't ever recall her being angry about anything. I'm not even sure she was capable of it. On my frequent visits, when it was time to go home, she'd always find a way to sneak love notes that she'd written to me into my pockets when we had our goodbye hug. To this day, I wonder how she knew exactly what I needed to hear, written painstakingly by her frail hands and then crisply folded and gingerly hidden in my pockets. I'm convinced she had her own special kind of magic. There's just no other way to explain it as no one ever witnessed her putting her love notes into our pockets.

Angela,

Stand strong, love endlessly and be yourself. I always love you! Grandma

I visited often when I was young and as I grew older I yearned for her touch and words of wisdom. I longed to be seen as only she could see me, at the depth of my soul. I knew there was something special about my Grandmother Nettie, looking back I miss the special way she carried love at her fingertips. With every word, every action, every touch she encompassed you with a heavenly sense of conscious love. The kind of pure love that is indescribable as it penetrates every cell of my being.

A large part of my childhood was spent on her front porch, sitting with her for hours in hard metal chairs facing the street, watching the traffic and people as they meandered by, saying hello and waving to every person that went past. No matter how old she got, grandma Nettie always looked at everything around her in amazement and wonder, the sort of thing we outgrow once we stop being a child. But Grandma Nettie never outgrew that. She exuded love and joy, and wanted to spread it to everyone around her.

She kept an open-door policy and everyone in our small town knew what that meant. There was a wooden front door of her house that she kept open and it soon became her symbol that meant you were always welcome to stop by to chat or have a cup of coffee. Grandma Nettie knew how to brighten everyone's day no matter what was going on in their lives.

Her skin was frail and thin yet with each touch of her hand I would melt into the warm tenderness of her essence. My Grandmother was very magnetic; people were naturally drawn to her. She always seemed to know what to say, and she chose her words carefully, fully knowing the value and power of each spoken word. She brought people joy and comfort, reminding them that they're loved and valuable. She saw something special in every single person, and had an uncanny knack for drawing out every person's unique gifts. My grandma Nettie bestowed healing onto those who needed it, through her touch, her words and her essence, and she always seemed to know who needed it.

She would make wise statements like, **"You are strong and you have the power to take hurt away from others, because you are capable of turning their hurt into love".** These wise statements would pop out of nowhere. They were especially on point even though I never spoke about my day or about how I was feeling. It's no wonder that after hearing these kinds of empowering statements growing up, I chose to become a counselor and healer, hoping to carry on at least some tiny fraction of Grandma Nettie's legacy. I like to think it would make her happy.

JUST KNOWING

She would read from the 'good book' and send forth information from it so you could apply it to your life. I remember listening to her read scripture one day when all of a sudden she gets up from the chair and moves closer to the phone, the kind of phone that hung from the wall. I asked her, "What are you doing?" She replied, "My sister Winnie is going to call soon." I asked her how she knew that and she would say, "I just know."

This internal knowing fascinated me, yet she never really spoke directly to it. When I would ask her how she knew things her reply was always the same, she "just knew." She shared this legacy of just knowing and as I grew older I found I "just knew" things as she used to. I have always taken these knowing's for granted as I assumed everyone had this sixth sense. I am so grateful my Grandmother taught me to listen and pay attention to these knowing's as they now lead my life.

Grandma Nettie's God like essence was prominent. She spoke of God often and how she communicated through her 'knowing.' When she spoke of God she spoke with conviction as if they were whole, wholeness in thought, in emotion, in being. Her relationship with her god-self inspired many as she had a sense of extreme calmness and she attributed it to her ability to know through listening to her truth.

Even though decades have passed, I still remember the day she died. The tears flowed like fountains, almost as if I was being emptied out. It was fitting, because some part of me felt empty without her in my life, without her loving touch, without her crystal blue eyes boring deep into my soul. Feelings of total loneliness pressed through to my bones as I told her goodbye, our very last goodbye. As the loneliness pressed into every cell of my body, searing deep into my bones, and leaving a dull, throbbing ache. I knew in that moment of our last goodbye that I was destined to follow her legacy.

As the days passed by my soul ached for her wisdom, her love, her beauty, her brilliance. I missed her zest for life, her taking delight in the simplest, everyday things. I missed the deep conversations we had about life. Little golden nuggets of consciousness would flow from her that were far beyond my years. Little did I know; those golden nuggets were tiny seeds she was planting and etching into every cell of every layer of my conscious being. There was a deep soul connection with my Grandmother that went beyond her gentleness, beyond her words and beyond this dimension. I knew I was to carry her legacy, planting seeds exceedingly, speaking of consciousness and intentional love helping to raise the vibration of this world.

My mother would comment about our relationship and how she saw something different and special about our connection. I had assumed it was because my Grandma Nettie spent so much time with my family, she recovered from two knee surgeries and stayed with us through my mother's heart attack. It was these days long ago that allowed us to grow close.

I don't believe I'll ever quite live up to Grandma Nettie and the legacy she left behind as it was her legacy. I can only grow the seeds she planted within me in her honor. But, I know deep within, our soul bond is stronger than death, and I know we're still connected. It's not even knowledge, really, it's something I can feel, what Grandma Nettie would call a "knowing". Every day of my life, I make a conscious effort to spread her message of joy, love and how to experience amazement about the simple wonders of the world. I feel Grandma Nettie's spirit with me all the time, as I know she helps to guide me in my quest for wisdom, love and joy.

WISDOM

As life passed by and my endless yearning to remember the heartfelt actions my Grandmother took every day with every person she knew lingered in my cells. As a counselor, I logically understand the grieving process, that each of us have our own special way of releasing the emotions of our memories of someone we love dearly. For 20 years, I grieved my grandmother, some of the most self-tormented moments of my life were spent wondering what she would say to me as my life experiences would pose questions of doubt and insecurity in my decisions.

One day as I was driving to an event of which I was a featured speaker, I asked my grandmothers spirit to give me some answers that would help others as well as myself. In my talk, I was using my grandmother's ability to "just know things" as an example of following your inner wisdom. There was not a day that went by when I would talk about her that I didn't break down in tears. I asked her spirit to help me move through my grief, my yearning for her to be present in my life. I wanted to make it through this speech without breaking down in tears and pleaded for answers.

I asked her spirit for guidance, to tell me what I needed to do to heal my tiresome feeling of missing her. Her spirit said, "What do you miss about me?" I thought for a moment and considered this a very valid question. What was it that I missed about her, what quality of her essence did I yearn for? It took a considerable amount of time before something came to me.

What I missed about my Grandmother Nettie was her unconditioned pure form of love. Never did I feel judged by her and she always understood who I was long before I did. She saw my soul as no one else did, not even myself. I longed for her beautiful words that always knew how to lift me up and would invoke some sort of confidence that came from deep within me. As I thought about this the tears began to flow and I heard my Grandmothers spirit say "Then become the things you miss about me. When you embody these qualities, you will no longer miss me."

Something profound happened to me in that moment, a deep sense of understanding the grieving process occurred. That day, during my speech I did not shed a tear. I spoke with ease and grace with a new sense of wisdom, a deep "knowing" that I had embodied the quality my heart yearned for. I became the essence of her.

I no longer miss my Grandmother, as I know I carry deep within my cells the seeds she planted within me years ago. I am thankful for all her teachings of how to be in life, pure love, wisdom and truth is how I live my life, just as she would have. I now sneak little love notes into pockets and leave them on store shelves for others to find. Here is one for you!

When you miss the presence of someone, remember the essence of what you miss. Then become that essence and you no longer miss them. You are very loved! Angela

About the Author

With over two decades of helping people make positive life changes, teaching, mentoring, speaking, writing and helping others find peace within is my life's mission.

The outcome of this work is an exciting blend of the academia of positive psychology, conscious conversations and the spirituality of the soul. As a consciousness mentor, I help people get crystal clear about beliefs, thoughts, emotions, words and actions, ultimately creating a sense of freedom through higher states of conscious awareness.

I am passionate about helping people through the ascension process as we create the New Earth of conscious love.

Webpage: http://angelablaha.com
Twitter: https://twitter.com/AngelaBlaha
Facebook: https://www.facebook.com/angela.blaha.9
https://www.facebook.com/angelablahapublic/
Instagram: https://www.instagram.com/angela_blaha/

VORACIOUSLY CURIOUS
THE ART OF DEEPENING CONNECTIONS
By: Kimi Avary

I climbed the stairs to the meet with my grandmother, Granny Nanny's, accountant Jim Avidesian, to pick up her will. I, being her caregiver, had been charged with retrieving it. She'd had a cerebral aneurism, and died peacefully in her sleep the night before. I know this because the sheets weren't tousled in the slightest, and although I'd never seen a dead body up close, I'd had an immediate sense from across the room that her spirit had left.

Jim greeted me immediately and solemnly. He had known my grandmother as Nancy Collins, and they had been friends for over 50 years. He handed me the enormous five-inch binder that encompassed her intentions for the people she loved who had been left behind.

In awe of the size, I opened it to find a small yellow sticky note right on top that read, "No funeral, but if you must, only invite my closest friends."

I looked at Jim, he cocked his head, and we both burst out laughing. It wasn't that she had a great sense of humor, it was the absurdity of the note because she always left people feeling heard and valued, and with the feeling that they were her dearest friend.

My Uncle Ned once told my dad, "I'm her favorite." My dad retorted, "She said I was her favorite!" The truth was that she only had favorites.

Everyone she'd ever met considered Granny Nanny their closest friend. I mean EVERYONE! My friends visited when I wasn't with them. My brother's friends visited. My cousin's friends visited. Even friends of friends visited. And so on.

For example, we'd had a massive surprise birthday party for her 69th and over 80 friends from around the world showed up. Including her ex-husband.

She connected with all kinds of people, different cultures, varying backgrounds, and all ages. She'd talk with an 8-year-old with the same ease an 80-year-old. For her, learning about others was a deeply joyful experience. She really truly only saw the goodness in all people.

It was unusual to visit her without running into a long-time family friend of some sort. These friends regularly joined us for family dinners. In fact, we have almost a century of dinner photos filled with friendly faces from her menagerie of friends. And of course, we always had an empty seat for the uninvited guest. That was her way.

The year before, my twin brothers, Eric and Arthur, and I were having our annual July birthday party at Granny Nanny's house in Menlo Park, California. We affectionately called it The Old House.

It was the house she'd grown up in, built in 1908 and purchased by my Great Grand Mother for a mere $2700. This Craftsman style house of aged redwood was filled with tiny French Windows that let in a quality of light rarely seen these days. Ancient and filled with memories the living room, dining room, and porch were all regularly filled with family and friends savoring connections; to love; to Granny Nanny.

Ever since we were little kids we'd had our birthday parties at the Old House. It was an exceptional place to have a celebration, because Granny Nanny was a master of them. Picture this, a five foot one inch "Grande Dame" with raven hair, brown eyes, a dashing smile, a whisky and water over ice in one hand, and a welcoming gesture with the other, exclaiming, "Oh Darling, it's so wonderful to see you!" She said this every time someone entered her home.

Granny Nanny exuded the commensurate Regal-ness of the Queen of Hearts opening her home and heart to the world, and we'd learned from her how to do parties right. We'd start at noon and go until 3 am.

This particular year was special because she'd fallen and broken one of her hips again. She'd had them both replaced about 10 years before, and at 88-years-old, she had decided not to do another surgery thus guaranteeing that she had no way of ever healing.

It meant to me that she was giving up and preparing to die. I remember how angry I was at first when she'd told me her decision. I begged and pleaded for her to do the surgery, but she was tired of her body that she felt had betrayed her with osteoporosis and osteoarthritis. She said, "I have the mind of a little girl in the body of a cracked crab."

I painfully and reluctantly understood. Especially after knowing how she'd lived her life as an incredibly vibrant person, and was now confined to her house, the use of a walker, and her granddaughter to take care of her. Although she had a steady stream of visitors, it was a far cry from the life she'd lived before.

I didn't officially work for her, because we'd found that arrangement undoable. I was the loving granddaughter, taking care of her Granny Nanny. I lived in the back cabin that her Grandfather "Gogi," Roger Marr Roberts, had built when he retired from Cornell University where he'd founded the School of Agriculture. I checked on her every morning, where she'd evaluate my work clothes, and I'd give her a massage every night before bed as I told her about my workday.

People trusted her. She was successful in pretty much everything that she did. In her business dealings, people liked to do business with her because she had the highest integrity, and it was fun to do business with her. She was always being offered deals that other people weren't offered just because people enjoyed having her in their partnerships.

She loved business and she'd worked for the same man, Raymond Handley, for over 50 years. On a plaque on the wall above his desk, he had this Loyalty Oath:

"TO WHOM IT MAY CONCERN and people it may not concern as well: I BELIEVE in and in the order as they appear: 1) Nancy Collins - my Grandmother 2) Renault & Handley 3) Nancy Pendleton 4) God 5) Ray Handley"

She didn't gain her boss' trust by being smart, which she was, or bossy, which she was. She gained it by being an incredible listener. She was genuinely curious about him and his business dealings. **She had the capacity to listen with such an intense interest, and so thoroughly that the people who encountered her felt truly seen.**

Near her room was a large round table where she loved to hold court. Today we would have called it the hang-out table. We'd played cards, dominos, dungeons and dragons, read books, and had long conversations there. Sometimes we'd casually dine there. It was the hub of our Old House activities.

From the round table, she could see the back yard, with numerous seating areas around a kidney shaped pool. It was the perfect perch for observing the lives of the people she cherished.

Since there was nothing we could do about changing her mind about opting out of another surgery, my brothers and I decided to make our party a tribute to Granny Nanny. We called everyone who had ever experienced her presence, and told them that this might be her last party with us, and invited them.

When the day came, hundreds of people showed up to visit with her. Granny Nanny donned in her favorite purple and white batik caftan with an amethyst broach on her neck, her hands adorned with her favorite large turquoise rings that camouflaged her arthritically crooked fingers, and sat elegantly at the round table as she received them all.

One person after the other sat with her and she listened with voracious curiosity as they shared the stories of their lives. Her gentle smile opened them up. Her nods and well-timed questions deepened their sharing. Her non-judgmental presence nourished their hearts.

This experience of being "seen" so deeply is rare. Especially in today's narcissistic world where most people selectively listen to others and focus only on what the conversation can do for them.

The disease of the day is Stuck in Your Own Head Syndrome, or SIYOHS for short, and although it's understandable, it's also prevalent. I don't think it's malicious. Instead, it's that we are so mired in technology that we are losing touch with how to have true connections.

We have over 950 trillion bits of information coming into our brains every single day; give or take a few. So, each and every one of us naturally deletes any seemingly irrelevant information, generalizes like-things into like-categories, and is victim to a distorted perception simply by not being curious about another person's experience.

If we didn't have these natural filtering mechanisms operating in our unconscious, the world would seem incredibly overwhelming. The challenge then is to consciously choose to be interested and curious about other people. To do that you must actually care about other people and their experience.

One of the things that Granny Nanny contributed to others was her voracious curiosity that was unattached to the outcome of their stories. To be voraciously curious means that you are choosing to listen to learn about another person, instead of half-hearted listening whilst you prepare what you're going to say. You refrain from interrupting, giving unsolicited advice, or correcting the speaker's viewpoint or opinion. It means that you are patient instead of rushing the speaker so you can have the floor.

Granny Nanny touched my heart and the hearts of so many others. She inspired voracious curiosity in me. She taught me how to listen and truly connect with others. That night as our party goers dispersed into the night, there was a satiated feeling that all was right with the world.

It is a precious gift to truly listen to another with deep curiosity. It lets them know that they are valuable and worthy of your attention. If you allow it to, it will broaden your world and make your life richer. It's a blessing for you and the speaker. This helps you connect deeply, lets people truly be seen, heard, and loved (or respected or celebrated) just as they are.

Listed below, please find my tips for living with Voracious Curiosity:

1. Create space in your life to listen to others (if you can't focus your attention right that moment, offer an alternate time)
2. Remember that your listening with Curiosity is a gift
3. Open your heart to receive the gift of another's experience
4. Be safe to speak to by softening your eyes and gently smile
5. Listen to learn about the other person

About the Author

Kimi Avary works with men and women who have challenges relating with each other both personally and professionally. She has been coaching for over 22 years, and working with couples to help them save their relationships since 2006. As a certified NLP (Neuro-Linguistic Programming) Master Practitioner, Kimi helps her clients bridge the gap between our thoughts, language and behavior to achieve greater success.

Kimi is a Licensed Relationship Coach and a PAX Programs Partner, she educates men and women about gender differences, the interaction of masculinity and femininity, and the principles of partnership. Her Masters in Counseling and Bachelor's Degree in Family Studies and Human Development provide her with a foundation to help men and women navigate and create the harmony they really want, personally and professionally.

She is the creator of the 90 Day Relationship Reboot Programs, the Relationship Navigation System, the Super Genius Teams

Program, and the Voraciously Curious 2 Day Workshop. Her upcoming book *The New Paradigm in Partnership* has been personally endorsed by Dr. John Gray of the Mars/Venus book series.

650-489-5346 office

650-714-4993 cell

http://kimiavary.com

http://ConsciousCouplesNetwork.com

http://VoraciouslyCurious.com

https://www.linkedin.com/in/kimiavary

http://twitter.com/kimiavary

http://facebook.com/ConsciousCouplesNetwork

http://www.youtube.com/ConsciousCouplesNet

MY LOVING LIGHT FILLED GRANDMOTHER
By: Barbara Gross

Today, I would like to honor my grandmother, Annie Rosen, as because of her light, I was shown the true meaning of unconditional love and to be able to laugh & enjoy life to its fullest!!!

Annie was born in 1892 in Russia and came to the USA in the early 1900s. She met and married Myer who also arrived in the USA about the same time. Myer and Annie had 2 daughters, 1st Lil and 6 years later, Esta. Lil married Eddie & had 2 boys & a girl. Esta married Benny & had 2 boys & a girl. My grandmother showed us the beauty & importance of always making sure that our families would stick together.

We always shared every holiday and birthday celebration together at my Aunt Lil & Eddie's house as they had a basement for parties. My father was a pioneer, as he bought a video camera that captured all our celebrations, minus the sound. Every chance our family got while together, we would watch our old home movies which were only of interest to us, but never bored us, as we could watch these movies time & time again to relive the moments.

But now let me tell you more about my personal relationship with the loving Grandmother, Annie. I don't know how many of you know the show, "The Beverly Hillbillies," but once I heard that family call their Grandmother, Granny, I started calling my Grandmother, "Granny", as well. I am just not the youngest from my immediate family but the youngest of our whole extended family.

Since I was so much younger than my siblings & cousins, by the time on came on the stage, I was known as "the baby". To this day, no matter how old I get, I am still "the baby." So, my grandmother became my best friend and played all sorts of games with me from picking the fastest raindrop, board games or card games. It seemed that every time I played cards with Granny, I would win!!! (I felt like a success!) I had no idea she was letting me win each time. One time Granny won by accident and she started to laugh uncontrollably. I really did not think this was funny & it hurt me deeply that my Granny would laugh at me. That was the day I found out I was not invincible and I was crushed, but in hindsight, it is hilarious!!!

We would go everywhere together as I just loved being with her. She always made me feel so special & let me know that I could do anything I set my mind to accomplishing so I always hoped she would be proud of me. I also watched how loving she was with everyone in our family. She was always right there to be supportive, for her family.

What I learned from her was to always be supportive, in any way I could, to help someone in need. I have been so blessed to know unconditional love and having the feeling around me of such security that I want to extend a hand to someone who did not have the benefit of my upbringing.

Once I was in junior high school, my mother started working during the day so when I came home from school, I would sit and watch the soap operas with Granny, and get involved with all of the characters. She had a hearing aid and for no apparent reason at random moments, it would give off this high pitched piercing sound. She could not hear it and I would have to shake her to tell her to fix it!!! Here I learned how to laugh at the unexpected as many things will happen in life and it is how you choose to react to every situation.

When she stayed overnight, she would put her teeth in a glass in the bathroom. I would also tease her if she ever lifted her arm wearing a sleeveless dress, as I would shake the loose skin below and she always laughed. I think if someone were to do that to me, I would get pretty irritated but not her. She taught me about intention as she knew I loved her and that, and was my way of being playful.

She could always make me laugh. One day shopping, she found a dress in a bag. Yes, that is how you bought it and a "big selling point." The dress was made of nylon material that you could roll up in a bag & when you opened the bag, the dress was perfect, not one wrinkle. She loved it!!! Here I learned that it doesn't matter what everyone else is wearing or doing but what suits you. It is really very fun and satisfying the more you can embrace your authentic self.

She knew me very well so she knew I was a very picky eater. When my Aunt Lil would have parties, she would have very nice food on the buffet table but I really liked little hotdogs and meatballs. I could not get enough of them and actually it was a lot cheaper that the other items on Lil's table. Well, one time Lil forgot to make my favorites and I started picking at her buffet table, and putting things back on the buffet table after I decided I didn't like it. When, new guests came to the buffet table and saw some of the piles of food I put back on her very organized, and fancy table, they were to say the least not very interested in tasting the food. Once, they figured out the culprit, I was taken away from the table, instead of getting angry at me, Granny said, "Lil, you should have made Barbara the hotdogs and meatballs." From then on, hotdogs and meatballs were always on the menu for me.

Speaking of meatballs, when I got my 1st puppy, he got sick and Granny thought that it would be a good idea to bind his stomach if he ate boiled meatballs. Of course, it was not the meat of the highest quality but they were meatballs and she made them for my sick puppy, and cured him. This filled me with joy as even though my Granny did not care for my puppy as much as I did, she would go out of her way to find a solution. She was always looking for the benefit of others and being so selfless. I was always in such awe of her and aspire to her virtues.

Once, I took a sewing class and let me just say, I knew early on that sewing was not going to be something I excelled at, however, I did make a nightgown for Granny, that hung a little crooked. She loved the fact that I made her a nightgown and to her it was perfect!!! **She wore it every night she slept over at our house and it would just make me laugh.**

I will just face the facts that I am not artistic when it comes to knitting, ceramics, painting (well, maybe I am okay with paint by numbers) but that did not matter to Granny as she thought everything I did was fantastic!!! If you have a choice to make someone feel better or worse about something with no real consequence, why not choose to make them feel better.

I was and can be a pretty good baker/cook when I want to be. She passed down some recipes that we still love to eat to this day. One of my favorites was potato pancakes. I would let you know the recipe but it is still a secret.

She attended every dance recital I had, as well as, was the 1st person to be in the car when I got my driver's license. She was not afraid. It would always fill my heart about how much I knew that she loved me and how much I loved her.

Granny died when was about 17 years old. I was just devastated. There are really no words to express my loss for the woman who was always on my side, no matter what!!! But at least she died peacefully in her sleep. I believe in quality of life and also making sure there are no words left unsaid; it was always love.

I once went to a psychic as a birthday present from some of my friends. I asked the psychic, "Since I was so close with my Granny, I was wondering when I hear a noise in my ears, does that mean that she is thinking of me?" The psychic closed her eyes for a moment as if to converse with my Granny and then replied, **"How could you even ask that question. Don't you know that for her the sun rose and set on you?" I just started to cry with joy.**

Each year that I get older, I have found myself to be more spiritual. My belief today is that we come into this life to learn a new virtue and to experience this life's sole purpose. I believe in this life that my soul purpose is to be able to show other people the gift to laugh at everyday living and be your true authentic self as my Grandmother had shown to me.

After all of these years have passed, to me, she has never left my side. I believe that she is watching me or is guiding me in my travels through life or could very well be connecting with me in this life in some other form.

I try to say the following affirmation as often as I can. I think this affirmation comes from the values extended to me from my family and especially from my Granny;

- I am unconditionally loved
- I am healthy
- I am wealthy
- I am successful
- I am happy
- I am my true authentic self
- I am grateful

…& then I pinch myself as that just makes me laugh!!! Remember to do something that will make you laugh! Carry the legacy of light, laughter and joy forward!

About the Author

I am from Massachusetts and after graduating college became a native Californian, however, my accent will have to be surgically removed.

My degree is in Education and I have been a teacher, but I am currently a Business Development Manager for Computer Software and I have been in the software industry since 1990. I have a Bachelor of Science in Education from the University of Massachusetts in Amherst, MA, President's Club Awards for Sales and Technical Expertise from Xerox Imaging Systems / Scan Soft and Vice President of Membership at ABBYY Talk ToastMasters Club in Milpitas, CA (4 years)

I would like to express my love for life by showing people how being able to laugh at oneself is great fun!!!

When people meet me, they ask me, "Why do all of these funny things happen to you???" and I reply, "If you listen carefully, they were not so funny at the time!!!"

I have learned that being my authentic self is what I want to be, and show others why that is valuable, as I have proven this to myself & others with the success I have achieved in life.

I think I have a story about almost any topic but below are some of my topics from my YouTube Videos: https://www.youtube.com/channel/UCTe05eh2e8D8-PLCOz-EFyw

Baaaaahston	My Boston Accent
Horseback Riding	Horseback Riding Stories
Embarrassing College	No Water, Drying Cleaning & Visiting
High Maintenance	Discuss Why I Am "The Director Of High Maintenance Women"
Pachos	Taking My Dog To The Veterinarian
Traveling	Mishaps While Traveling
Birthday Shirts	Funny Birthday Party

blgross@sbcglobal.net

https://www.facebook.com/barbara.gross.9047

https://www.facebook.com/baaaaahbra/

https://twitter.com/baaaaahbra

https://www.linkedin.com/in/barbaralgross

https://www.youtube.com/channel/UCTe05eh2e8D8-PLCOz-EFyw

HOMESTEADING IN NORTH DAKOTA
By: Sandra Edwards

My Grandma Sims always made the best of what she had. She always had a smile and good things to say of everyone. She was happy and you just had to happy with her. She never stopped moving and she never complained. She loved unconditionally. That is the legacy I take from my Grandma Sims. Work hard, love what you do, judge no one, be present and alive every day.

I first remember my Grandma Sims in the little house with the white picket fence in Williston North Dakota. She had plants growing everywhere. There were lilacs in the spring, hollyhocks in the summer and rhubarb outside the kitchen door. My sister and I loved sitting out on the steps with rhubarb and sugar to dip it in. That was the greatest. Cold frosts come pretty early in the fall so some plants would go into the house filling up the living room and most are left to the freezing weather.

Grandma had a way with plants. I guess they thrived on her love and attention. She had a philodendron plant that grew all the way around her kitchen several times. The local newspaper came and took pictures of her plant and interviewed her. She loved African violets and they were everywhere in her house.

Grandpa and Grandma Sims, their names were Odus and Minnie, moved to this little house in Williston from the homestead about 60 miles south west, almost to the Montana border, in the 1940's.

As a young woman Grandma came from Minnesota in the early 1900's. Her two brothers were already in North Dakota on their homesteads and they convinced her to come and have her own homestead. When I think of it I just can't understand how Grandma got along in the harsh climate - the cold and blizzardy winters, and the glaring hot summers. She was 20 miles from the little community and 40 miles from a community large enough to have a doctor with only horses for transportation. Of-course there was no telephones at time.

Her brothers both died during the flu epidemic not too long after Grandma got settled on her homestead. Now she was really alone. But not truly alone, as it turns out Odus, Grandpa Sims had the homestead next to Grandma's. Eventually they got married and had five children, Vivian, Lillian, Ford and Betty. One child, Iris, died of a ruptured appendix at age five. The loss of that child was very traumatic for the family, especially Ford as he had a special affinity for Iris. They were close in age and best friends. Ford later named one of his own daughters Iris.

Life at this time on the homestead taught me so much about appreciating for running water, and other amenities we take for granted. The hand pump drew water from the well for drinking and for washing and laundry. The bathroom was quite a walk from the house - two holes with catalog paper.

I know the house well as we lived there a lot after our Grandparents moved to Williston. It was very small with a little food pantry and an iron cook stove with a reservoir for hot water. The cook stove was the only heat; hard to think what it was like in the winter.

There was an upstairs room, the stairs were steep and the room was small with a slanted ceiling. The chimney of the stove was next to the stairs and up through the room. All the children stayed in that little room. My sister, Gloria, and I stayed in that room too and found it hard to imagine that Grandma's five children could live in that tiny space. We found their names carved in the chimney bricks making their childhood longings and dreams so real to us. I really appreciate the legacy of survival and perseverance.

The house sat on the edge of the badlands. There were no trees or shelter. Just a teeny uninsulated house standing there by itself exposed to all kinds of extreme weather. Coal was used for cooking and for heat. Horses and sleds were taken into the badlands to bring back the precious coal.

During the summer, especially late summer, they had crews of men helping with the harvest. Grandma had to feed them. I can't imagine how she put together enough food to feed a large group of men day after day. She would bake pies for them, in her tiny kitchen area. I think by that time the oldest daughter helped her in the kitchen. It must have been good training because that daughter, Vivian, later ran cafes and other eateries. This legacy of being creative, the ability to serve many continues on.

Lillian and Ford did more of the outside chores. They rode their horses to check on the cattle, milked the cows and cleaned the barns. And the fencing, there were always fences to be built and to mend.

The children all worked hard continuing this legacy of valuing hard work. There was no playing. If they had spare time they picked rock - there were always rocks to pick. Each year the winter freeze would push the rock to the surface and they needed to be picked and stacked out of the way of the machines.

The school house was one room and was several miles away. They walked the distance no matter the weather. Ford had a horse but he was not sharing rides to school.

I remember hearing a story about Grandpa selling Grandma's horse. Horses were all important at that time and this horse had been a gift from Grandma's family in Minnesota. She loved that horse and Grandpa sold it without telling her. She was furious at him. That is the challenge of two independent people coming together. I am not sure how they worked it out, but survival issues on the homestead must have kept them going. I appreciate the legacy of keeping on track no matter what.

During the winter, they would have a rope from the house to the barn so they could get to the barn safely to care for the animals during blizzards. They must have had a rope to the outhouse too as it was quite a distance from the house.

Sometimes in the winter they would take the horse and sled down to the creek and carve out some ice. The ice was taken back to the house to make ice cream. Wow, what a treat, ice cream! A well-deserved treat for all their hard work. Ice cream is a family celebration for which no money is spent. Money is spent for the important necessities like shoes and tools, grain to feed the animals or to plant. Clothes were handed down from one child to the next. The legacy about conserving money has passed down through the generations. A legacy I am always thankful for.

There was a root cellar to keep food through the winter. Eggs and meat packed in lard, vegetables and fruit in jars. They only had the summer to do all the work because winters were frozen solid with no food to be found and it was a long way to the store even if they did have the money.

Although moving to Williston must have been a real luxury for Grandma compared to the homestead, they took in roomers in the basement and Grandma did their laundry getting paid very little for doing that. I remember helping Grandma run the clothes through the wringer and hanging them on the line. Even with running water and electricity it was hard work. Guess Grandma thrived on hard work. She couldn't be still - had to be doing something all the time.

Grandma was very frugal. I remember going to Williston to stay with her and my Mother had given me two quarters which I had put into the suitcase I was carrying. When I unpacked, the quarters were not there. I couldn't find them, but Grandma would not let it go. She went through that suitcase with a fine-toothed comb and finally found the quarters stuck in the lining of the suitcase.

Christmas Day at Grandma and Grandpa's was the tradition. The finest dishware came out. They were square shaped and creamy colored with gold design. They ordered all the fine things from Sears and Roebuck after moving to Williston. All of their kids were there for the celebration with all their kids. It was quite a group. Grandma made all the food which was wonderfully delicious-krumkake, rosettes, lefse; all Swedish traditions.

She loved to bake and she was known for her doughnuts. I remember a pie, a pumpkin chiffon pie. I recently found her recipe and plan to see how I do with it. I know it will not be like Grandma's. I remember Grandma's long hair; so long she could actually sit on it. She wore it in a braid wrapped around her head. When she developed severe headaches, she had to cut it off, it was too heavy for her to carry anymore. The long braid lay in a dresser drawer until she died. She also had bursitis and she had to stretch her arms up regularly to stay mobile. I helped her do that, taking each arm and pushing upward. She said it was better when I helped her because grandpa was a little rough. I wonder how she did that after Grandpa died.

Hoop skirts were all the rage when I was in my early teens. Many adults complained they were so silly and unpractical, but not Grandma Sims. She was always an advocate for the latest thing, always wanting to know what was going on in the world.

I remember sitting in the chair by the window while she was putting a pie together. I asked why she was doing that and she told me that Grandpa liked it - she was baking for Grandpa and she really loved doing that.

They loved each other and it was good seeing them together. When Grandpa died, she made an effort to let all the grandchildren know how much he had enjoyed them. He was not a demonstrative man so maybe she wanted to speak for him.

The last years of her life she was going around to the old folk's homes to visit her friends, taking them little gifts and keeping their spirits up. Grandma stayed in her own home to the end. She and the other ladies in the neighborhood had an agreement. In the morning when getting up they would put up their window shade to let everyone know they were ok. I appreciate her practical and creative approach to life and community.

The last time I saw Grandma she came to visit us in Helena, Montana. Grandma was always so alive, so present it was such a pleasure to be with her. I remember that my brother, Steven, had some kind of little motor bike or was it a big motorcycle. What I do remember is that Grandma rode behind Steven and she was having the time of her life.

The message came. Grandma had been hanging clothes on the clothes line outside the back door, she came into the house and laid down on the bed in the little bedroom and died with a smile on her face. She was 73 years old.

Here is the wisdom and legacy Grandma Sims shared in my life that I would like to share with you.
1. Work hard and conserve money
2. Love what you do
3. Judge no one
4. Be present and alive every day
5. Love unconditionally

About the Author

Sandra Edwards is a certified intuitive Hand Analyst. She focuses on life purpose discovery and personality style rather than prediction of the future. Helping people through life transitions has been Sandra's focus and mission for more than 40 years, beginning with a 30-year career helping people through their divorce process, and now as a Hand Analyst with guidance based on the information in their own hands.
Sandra@sandrareadshands.com
www.Facebook.com/SandraReadsHands
www.sandrareadshands.com

THANK YOU NOTE FROM THE COMPILER

Dear Powerful Reader,

Thank you for reading our anthology. I hope it has touched your heart and spirit; encouraging and inspiring you. We hope these powerful legacy stories inspire you to step into your own legacy stories and SHINE!

I wanted to share a little bit more about our organizations, Your Purpose Driven Practice™ and RHG Media Productions™. We are passionate about helping others live on purpose and with purpose in their life and business. I hope this book has supported and inspired you to choose to live on purpose, bloom and SHINE!

If you're wanting or needing to reach more people and be part of inspiring and supporting others with your message, your gifts, and the work that you bring to the world; then I wanted to share some opportunities for you to consider.

Each year we compile and produce multiple anthology book projects, produce and publish an international magazine, launch TV shows, facilitate women's empowerment conferences, launch radio and podcast shows, help experts and speakers step into a place of powerful influence to make a global difference.

We provide programs and strategies to help you reach more people, and facilitate the Speaker Talent Search (which helps speakers, experts, and influencers connect with more speaking opportunities.) We would love to support you in reaching more people. Please take a moment to learn a little bit more about us at the sites listed below, and then reach out to us for a conversation. **We would love to have you join us as we seek to make a positive global difference; one heart and life at a time.**

You can learn more about each of these things are our main website: www.YourPurposeDrivenPractice.com

Enjoy our powerful TV programs: www.RHGTVNetwork.com

Learn more about the Speaker Talent Search™: www.SpeakerTalentSearch.com

If you would like to connect with me personally to explore some of our opportunities in upcoming book projects, podcast/radio shows, and/or TV, then here is the link to schedule a time to speak with me directly: www.MeetWithRebecca.com or you can email me at: Rebecca@YourPuposeDrivenPractice.com

May you always choose to share your Legacy!

Warmly,
Rebecca Hall Gruyter

CLOSING THOUGHTS

I hope you have been touched by these powerful legacies stories and messages in this book. We hope you have been encouraged on your journey and are inspired to apply the wisdom that touched your heart and spirit...and to be willing to share your legacy stories... We can't wait to see you, hear from you, and celebrate you as you share the gift of you with the world!

We wanted to share about some additional books Rebecca is part of and some upcoming books that you may also enjoy that we are excited to be publishing.

*Books compiled or written by Rebecca Hall Gruyter to be released in 2018:

Empowering You, Transforming Lives, this anthology features over 50 powerful experts coming together to give you support 365 days a year.

Real time support, inspiration and reflection each, and every day of the year; it was also have a special section in the back where you can look up by subject the area you are looking for support, encouragement or wisdom in throughout the year and throughout your life.

We believe this book will be one that refer to again and again as it walks beside you in practical and profound way to help you live a powerful and empowering life! (To be released in late November/early December 2018.)

Step Forward and SHINE! This anthology featuring over 25 authors (the third book in the SHINE series) will empower readers to discover the actions they can take to move forward and SHINE in the areas that matter most to them. The world needs you NOW! (To be released in August/September of 2018).

*Books Featuring a Chapter/Section by Rebecca Hall Gruyter to be released in 2018:

"**The Power of Our Voices, Sharing Our Story**" Anthology, compiled by Teresa Hawley-Howard

"**40/40**" Anthology, compiled by Holly Porter

"**Keep Smiling, Shift Happens'** Special Keep Smiling Movement Special VoiceAmerica™ Edition featuring VoiceAmerica™ Radio Show Hosts, Anthology, compiled by Dr. Emily Letran and Ken Rochon, JR.

Books Previously Released and available on Amazon *(Books compiled by Rebecca or featuring a chapter or foreword written by Rebecca Hall Gruyter):*

Compiled by Rebecca:

First 2 Books in the 3-Part SHINE Series:

"**Come Out of Hiding and SHINE!**" Anthology compiled by Rebecca Hall Gruyter

"**Bloom Where You Are Planted and SHINE!**" Anthology compiled by Rebecca Hall Gruyter

---

Featuring a Chapter/Foreword Written by Rebecca Hall Gruyter:

"**Becoming Outrageously Successful**" Anthology compiled by Dr. Anita Jackson

"**Catch Your Star**" Anthology published by THRIVE Publishing

"**Discover Your Destiny**" Anthology compiled by Denise Joy Thompson

"**I Am Beautiful**" Anthology compiled by Teresa Hawley-Howard

"**Succeeding Against All Odds**" Anthology compiled by Sandra Yancey

"**Success Secrets for Today's Feminine Entrepreneurs: Secrets from Today's Top Feminine Leaders on Fulfillment, Satisfaction, and Abundance**" Anthology compiled by Dr. Anita Jackson

"**Unstoppable Woman of Purpose**" Anthology and workbook, compiled by Nella Chikwe

"**Warrior Women Who Make It Rock: Transformational Stories of Love, Power, and Respect**" Anthology compiled by Nichole Peters

"**Women of Courage, Women of Destiny: Moving From Fear to Faith to Freedom** Anthology compiled by Dr. Anita Jackson

"**Women on a Mission**" Anthology compiled by Teresa Hawley-Howard

"**You Are Whole, Perfect, and Complete - Just As You Are**" compiled by Carol Plummer and Susan Driscoll

Reviews

Marlene Elizabeth
Financial Spirituality Coach
www.marleneelizabeth.com

"A wealth of beautiful, rich, powerful messages infused with deep elder-wisdom for healing, strength, courage, compassion, forgiveness and triumph! These treasured legacy stories left me feeling goose-bumps, tears, giggles, love and a greater admiration for my grandma and grandmothers everywhere. I'm truly inspired by the life lessons, inspiration and encouragement on everything from self-care to overcoming deep challenges and living with purpose, along with helpful legacy tips.

As one author stated about her grandmother, "I marvel at her brave heart and how at mid-life she chose not to resign herself to a life of quiet misery and instead chose to allow for more love, more joy, more freedom, more living." You will LOVE this book! I can't wait to share it as a gift with my beloved grandmother and daughter.

Denise Hansard
Life Architect & Motivational Speaker
http://denisehansard.com

Inspiring! Truth! Strength! All of this is found within the Grandmother Legacies!

This book captures so beautifully the wisdom of our lineage, the history of our suffering & survival, and the beautiful, strong, empowered women we have become ... connected as one growing together.

The beauty of our Grandmothers' Legacies will speak to you having you share your own stories to be passed down, captured and continued as your legacy.

Tresté Loving
CEO/Founder
Institute for Racial Equity
www.tiredofhate.com

Beautiful Secrets!

This compilation is amazing, healthy, and beyond insightful. The rich diversity of race and ethnicity makes it interesting and very appropriate for our global community. Spotlighting the tenacious, strong, intelligent, resourceful spirit of a woman is long overdue and this book is right on the mark.

We, as women, rarely look at our lives as a legacy for our families. This book is does an excellent job of showing us how to live our lives out loud and to pass that on to all those who come after us! You must explore this book.

Carolyn CJ Jones
Resentment and Forgiveness Specialist/Guide
www.carolyncjjones.com

From the beginning, these legacies spoke to me. It was not only the courage, hope, and wisdom of the Grandmothers, it was these traits that I saw in each author, as well. Even further, this book led me to contemplate my own grandmothers; I was never close to either because we lived a distance away.

I have been given a new lens through which to look, due to this book. Truly, I resonated from the beginning with wisdom like, "… no accidental people on Earth," "work hard, love what you do, judge no one, be present and alive every day," and we "… can develop wisdom from suffering."

These and countless truths and nuggets that appear throughout *The Grandmother Legacies* enrich my practice of self-awareness and spirituality. I am deeply touched and impressed with the level of depth reflected in these pages and believe *The Grandmother Legacies* will touch the heart and soul of each who reads it. We will become a better world for that. Beautiful work, authors. Thank you.

Linda Patten
Leadership Expert
www.dare2dreamwithlinda.com

Like so many momentous roles in our lives, i.e. marriage, having that first child, becoming a leader, there are no manuals to teach us how to be that perfect, or even imperfect, grandmother.

Rebecca Hall Gruyter has brought together women with amazing stories about their journey. My expectation of what this book would teach me, would cause me to look deeply into and would inspire me was high as I have worked with Rebecca on many projects. I can tell you that this book did not disappoint in those areas and far more.

The stories are poignant, heart-felt, nostalgic and touching. The authors were authentic in the telling of their legacy tales and brought in elements of fun and joy as well as compassion and wonder. At times, I was laughing with the author and sometimes there were tears as I remembered my own Grandmother stories. This book of deeply felt stories should be a "must" for every woman as she becomes a mother or a grandmother, as she looks back at the legacy her grandmother(s) gave to her, or as she needs inspiration during all the times of her life. Read it, Experience it, Embrace it!

Carmell Pelly
Coach for the soul
www.carmellpelly.com

The Grandmother Legacies is a heartwarming, beautifully written book that will cause you to feel lighter and put a smile on your face.

As I read chapter after chapter (having a hard time putting it down) I could not help but reflect on my own experiences with my grandmother, including several that had been forgotten.

This book is an amazing reminder of the importance that our grandmothers have in our lives and I absolutely love how every author has put their heart and soul into their writing their story.

Syndee Hendricks
www.SyndeeHendricks.com
www.ImagineMoreSuccess.com

What a wonderful experience to have so many of my own grandmother special love and life-long memories rekindled while reading this remarkably special writing. With so many similarities of my own familial experiences throughout this lovely work, I couldn't help but embrace many of the fascinating stories of life, love, hope, and struggle from those first US generations. Especially extraordinary was to read of some of our country's history as well as world history through the eyes of the families who lived it.

It was enlightening to also learn of how other families survived many of the last century's challenges as my only grandmother whom I knew into my adulthood scaled like a man. While working in a man's world in the 1930's – 1970s, she shared her big lesson with me years later—and I'll share it with you: "You can always be a lady in a man's world, Syndee! Remember that" And, I have.

The Grandmother Legacies is so much more that a memoir of mothers and granddaughters that I am sure you will not be able to put it down as the memories, world history, and poignant moments will inspire you.

Janice Edwards

Edwards Host & Executive Producer "Bay Area Vista"
President & CEO, Edwards Unlimited
bayareavista.com

In this season, when the focus is on giving, The Grandmother Legacies, is a true treasure that will continue to give for years to come.

The rich stories of faith, determination, and the imprint that these powerful and courageous women left in their granddaughters' hearts and souls, as well as in the world, are truly inspirational. It reminded me of the life lessons from my own beloved grandmothers, and it encourages all of us to sow a fruitful, positive and lasting legacy into the lives of those we know.

Thank you, Rebecca Hall Gruyter and authors, you have blessed us with this book.

www.ingramcontent.com/pod-product-compliance
Lightning Source LLC
Chambersburg PA
CBHW071925290426
44110CB00013B/1484